Harvard Business Review

ON

MARKETING

THE HARVARD BUSINESS REVIEW PAPERBACK SERIES

The series is designed to bring today's managers and professionals the fundamental information they need to stay competitive in a fast-moving world. From the preeminent thinkers whose work has defined an entire field to the rising stars who will redefine the way we think about business, here are the leading minds and landmark ideas that have established the *Harvard Business Review* as required reading for ambitious businesspeople in organizations around the globe.

Other books in the series:

Harvard Business Review Interviews with CEOs

Harvard Business Review on Advances in Strategy

Harvard Business Review on Brand Management

Harvard Business Review on Breakthrough Leadership

Harvard Business Review on Breakthrough Thinking

Harvard Business Review on Business and the Environment

Harvard Business Review on the Business Value of IT

Harvard Business Review on Change

Harvard Business Review on Compensation

Harvard Business Review on Corporate Governance

Harvard Business Review on Corporate Strategy

Harvard Business Review on Crisis Management

Harvard Business Review on Culture and Change

Harvard Business Review on Customer Relationship Management

Harvard Business Review on Decision Making

Harvard Business Review on Effective Communication

Harvard Business Review on Entrepreneurship

Harvard Business Review on Finding and Keeping the Best People

Harvard Business Review on Innovation

Harvard Business Review on Knowledge Management

Harvard Business Review

ON

MARKETING

A HARVARD BUSINESS REVIEW PAPERBACK

The *Harvard Business Review* articles in this collection are available as
individual reprints. Discounts apply to quantity purchases. For information and ordering, please contact Customer Service, Harvard Business
School Publishing, Boston, MA 02163. Telephone: (617) 783-7500 or
(800) 988-0886, 8 A.M. to 6 P.M. Eastern Time, Monday through Friday.
Fax: (617) 783-7555, 24 hours a day. E-mail: custserv@hbsp.harvard.edu

Library of Congress Control Number: 2002100251

*The paper used in this publication meets the requirements of the Ameri-
can National Standard for Permanence of Paper for Publications and
Documents in Libraries and Archives Z39.48-1992.*

Contents

Harvard
Business
Review

ON

MARKETING

The Brand Report Card

KEVIN LANE KELLER

Executive Summary

MOST MANAGERS RECOGNIZE the value in building
and properly managing a brand. But few can objectively
assess their brand's particular strengths and weaknesses.
Most have a good sense of one or two areas in which
their brand may excel or may need help. But, if pressed,
many would find it difficult even to identify all the factors
they should be considering.

To give managers a systematic way to think about
their brands, Tuck School professor Kevin Lane Keller
lays out the ten characteristics that the strongest brands
share. He starts with the relationship of the brand to the
customer: The strongest brands excel at delivering the
benefits customers truly desire, he says. They stay relevant to customers over time. Pricing truly reflects consumers' perceptions of value.

Keller then moves on to consider marketing strategy and implementation: Strong brands are properly positioned. The brand stays consistent. Subbrands relate to one another in an orderly way within a portfolio of brands. A full range of marketing tools are employed to build brand equity.

Finally, he looks at management considerations: Mangers of strong brands understand what the brand means to customers. The company gives the brand proper support and sustains it over the long term. And the company consistently measures sources of brand equity.

By grading a brand according to how well it addresses each dimension, managers can come up with a comprehensive brand report card. By doing the same for competitors' brands, they can gain a fuller understanding of the relative strengths of their own brands in the marketplace.

BUILDING AND PROPERLY MANAGING brand equity has become a priority for companies of all sizes, in all types of industries, in all types of markets. After all, from strong brand equity flow customer loyalty and profits. The rewards of having a strong brand are clear.

The problem is, few managers are able to step back and assess their brand's particular strengths and weaknesses objectively. Most have a good sense of one or two areas in which their brand may excel or may need help. But if pressed, many (understandably) would find it difficult even to identify all of the factors they should be considering. When you're immersed in the day-to-day management of a brand, it's not easy to keep in perspective all the parts that affect the whole.

In this article, I'll identify the ten characteristics that the world's strongest brands share and construct a brand report card—a systematic way for managers to think about how to grade their brand's performance for each of those characteristics. The report card can help you identify areas that need improvement, recognize areas in which your brand is strong, and learn more about how your particular brand is configured. Constructing similar report cards for your competitors can give you a clearer picture of their strengths and weaknesses. One caveat: Identifying weak spots for your brand doesn't necessarily mean identifying areas that need more attention. Decisions that might seem straightforward—"We haven't paid much attention to innovation: let's direct more resources toward R&D"—can sometimes prove to be serious mistakes if they undermine another characteristic that customers value more.

The Top Ten Traits

The world's strongest brands share these ten attributes:

1. **The brand excels at delivering the benefits customers truly desire.** Why do customers really buy a product? Not because the product is a collection of attributes but because those attributes, together with the brand's image, the service, and many other tangible and intangible factors, create an attractive whole. In some cases, the whole isn't even something that customers know or can say they want.

Consider Starbucks. It's not just a cup of coffee. In 1983, Starbucks was a small Seattle-area coffee retailer. Then while on vacation in Italy, Howard Schultz, now Starbucks chairman, was inspired by the romance and the sense of community he felt in Italian coffee bars and coffee houses. The culture grabbed him, and he saw an opportunity.

"It seemed so obvious," Schultz says in the 1997 book he wrote with Dori Jones Yang, *Pour Your Heart Into It.* "Starbucks sold great coffee beans, but we didn't serve coffee by the cup. We treated coffee as produce, something to be bagged and sent home with the groceries. We stayed one big step away from the heart and soul of what coffee has meant throughout centuries."

And so Starbucks began to focus its efforts on building a coffee bar culture, opening coffee houses like those in Italy. Just as important, the company maintained control over the coffee from start to finish—from the selection and procurement of the beans to their roasting and blending to their ultimate consumption. The extreme vertical integration has paid off. Starbucks locations thus far have successfully delivered superior benefits to customers by appealing to all five senses—through the enticing aroma of the beans, the rich taste of the coffee, the product displays and attractive artwork adorning the walls, the contemporary music playing in the background, and even the cozy, clean feel of the tables and chairs. The company's startling success is evident: The average Starbucks customer visits a store 18 times a month and spends $3.50 a visit. The company's sales and profits have each grown more than 50% annually through much of the 1990s.

2. The brand stays relevant. In strong brands, brand equity is tied both to the actual quality of the product or service and to various intangible factors. Those intangibles include "user imagery" (the type of person who uses the brand); "usage imagery" (the type of situations in which the brand is used); the type of personality the brand portrays (sincere, exciting, competent, rugged);

the feeling that the brand tries to elicit in customers (purposeful, warm); and the type of relationship it seeks to build with its customers (committed, casual, seasonal). Without losing sight of their core strengths, the strongest brands stay on the leading edge in the product arena and tweak their intangibles to fit the times.

Gillette, for example, pours millions of dollars into R&D to ensure that its razor blades are as technologically advanced as possible, calling attention to major advances through subbrands (Trac II, Atra, Sensor, Mach3) and signaling minor improvements with modifiers (Atra Plus, SensorExcel). At the same time, Gillette has created a consistent, intangible sense of product superiority with its long-running ads, "The best a man can be," which are tweaked through images of men at work and at play that have evolved over time to reflect contemporary trends.

These days, images can be tweaked in many ways other than through traditional advertising, logos, or slogans. "Relevance" has a deeper, broader meaning in today's market. Increasingly, consumers' perceptions of a company as a whole and its role in society affect a brand's strength as well. Witness corporate brands that very visibly support breast cancer research or current educational programs of one sort or another.

3. The pricing strategy is based on consumers' perceptions of value. The right blend of product quality, design, features, costs, and prices is very difficult to achieve but well worth the effort. Many managers are woefully unaware of how price can and should relate to what customers think of a product, and they therefore charge too little or too much.

For example, in implementing its value-pricing strategy for the Cascade automatic-dishwashing detergent brand, Procter & Gamble made a cost-cutting change in its formulation that had an adverse effect on the product's performance under certain—albeit somewhat atypical—water conditions. Lever Brothers quickly countered, attacking Cascade's core equity of producing "virtually spotless" dishes out of the dishwasher. In response, P&G immediately returned to the brand's old formulation. The lesson to P&G and others is that value pricing should not be adopted at the expense of essential brand-building activities.

By contrast, with its well-known shift to an "everyday low pricing" (EDLP) strategy, Procter & Gamble did successfully align its prices with consumer perceptions of its products' value while maintaining acceptable profit levels. In fact, in the fiscal year after Procter & Gamble switched to EDLP (during which it also worked very hard to streamline operations and lower costs), the company reported its highest profit margins in 21 years.

4. The brand is properly positioned. Brands that are well positioned occupy particular niches in consumers' minds. They are similar to and different from competing brands in certain reliably identifiable ways. The most successful brands in this regard keep up with competitors by creating *points of parity* in those areas where competitors are trying to find an advantage while at the same time creating *points of difference* to achieve advantages over competitors in some other areas.

The Mercedes-Benz and Sony brands, for example, hold clear advantages in product superiority and match competitors' level of service. Saturn and Nordstrom lead their respective packs in service and hold their own in quality. Calvin Klein and Harley-Davidson excel at providing compelling user and usage imagery while offering adequate or even strong performance.

Visa is a particularly good example of a brand whose managers understand the positioning game. In the 1970s and 1980s, American Express maintained the high-profile brand in the credit card market through a series of highly effective marketing programs. Trumpeting that "membership has its privileges," American Express came to signify status, prestige, and quality.

In response, Visa introduced the Gold and the Platinum cards and launched an aggressive marketing campaign to build up the status of its cards to match the American Express cards. It also developed an extensive merchant delivery system to differentiate itself on the basis of superior convenience and accessibility. Its ad campaigns showcased desirable locations such as famous restaurants, resorts, and events

Maintaining a strong brand means striking the right balance between continuity and change.

that did not accept American Express while proclaiming, "Visa. It's everywhere you want to be." The aspirational message cleverly reinforced both accessibility and prestige and helped Visa stake out a formidable position for its brand. Visa became the consumer card of choice for family and personal shopping, for personal travel and entertainment, and even for international travel, a former American Express stronghold.

Of course, branding isn't static, and the game is even more difficult when a brand spans many product categories. The mix of points of parity and point of difference that works for a brand in one category may not be quite right for the same brand in another.

5. The brand is consistent. Maintaining a strong brand means striking the right balance between continuity in marketing activities and the kind of change needed to stay relevant. By continuity, I mean that the brand's image doesn't get muddled or lost in a cacophony of marketing efforts that confuse customers by sending conflicting messages.

Just such a fate befell the Michelob brand. In the 1970s, Michelob ran ads featuring successful young professionals that confidently proclaimed, "Where you're going, it's Michelob." The company's next ad campaign trumpeted, "Weekends were made for Michelob." Later, in an attempt to bolster sagging sales, the theme was switched to "Put a little weekend in your week." In the mid-1980s, managers launched a campaign telling consumers that "The night belongs to Michelob." Then in 1994 we were told, "Some days are better than others," which went on to explain that "A special day requires a special beer." That slogan was subsequently changed to "Some days were made for Michelob."

Pity the poor consumers. Previous advertising campaigns simply required that they look at their calendars or out a window to decide whether it was the right time to drink Michelob; by the mid-1990s, they had to figure out exactly what kind of day they were having as well. After receiving so many different messages, consumers could hardly be blamed if they had no idea when they were supposed to drink the beer. Predictably, sales suffered. From a high in 1980 of 8.1 million barrels, sales dropped to just 1.8 million barrels by 1998.

Boundaries are important. Overlapping two brands in the same portfolio can be dangerous.

6. The brand portfolio and hierarchy make sense. Most companies do not have only one brand; they create and maintain different brands for different market segments. Single product lines are often sold under different brand names, and different brands within a company hold different powers. The corporate, or companywide, brand acts as an umbrella. A second brand name under that umbrella might be targeted at the family market. A third brand name might nest one level below the family brand and appeal to boys, for example, or be used for one type of product.

Brands at each level of the hierarchy contribute to the overall equity of the portfolio through their individual ability to make consumers aware of the various products and foster favorable associations with them. At the same time, though, each brand should have its own boundaries; it can be dangerous to try to cover too much ground with one brand or to overlap two brands in the same portfolio.

The Gap's brand portfolio provides maximum market coverage with minimal overlap. Banana Republic anchors the high end, the Gap covers the basic style-and-quality terrain, and Old Navy taps into the broader mass market. Each brand has a distinct image and its own sources of equity.

BMW has a particularly well-designed and implemented hierarchy. At the corporate brand level, BMW pioneered the luxury sports sedan category by combining seemingly incongruent style and performance considerations. BMW's clever advertising slogan, "The ultimate driving machine," reinforces the dual aspects of this image and is applicable to all cars sold under the BMW name. At the same time, BMW created well-differentiated subbrands through its 3, 5, and 7 series, which suggest a logical order and hierarchy of quality and price.

General Motors, by contrast, still struggles with its brand portfolio and hierarchy. In the early 1920s, Alfred P. Sloan decreed that his company would offer "a car for every purse and purpose." This philosophy led to the creation of the Cadillac, Oldsmobile, Buick, Pontiac, and Chevrolet divisions. The idea was that each division would appeal to a unique market segment on the basis of price, product design, user imagery, and so forth. Through the years, however, the marketing overlap among the five main GM divisions increased, and the divisions' distinctiveness diminished. In the mid-1980s, for example, the company sold a single body type (the J-body) modified only slightly for the five different brand names. In fact, advertisements for Cadillac in the 1980s actually stated that "motors for a Cadillac may come from other divisions, including Buick and Oldsmobile."

In the last ten years, the company has attempted to sharpen the divisions' blurry images by repositioning each brand. Chevrolet has been positioned as the value-priced, entry-level brand. Saturn represents no-haggle customer-oriented service. Pontiac is meant to be the sporty, performance-oriented brand for young people. Oldsmobile is the brand for larger, medium-priced cars. Buick is the premium, "near luxury" brand. And Cadillac, of course, is still the top of the line. Yet the goal remains challenging. The financial performance of Pontiac and Saturn has improved. But the top and bottom lines have never regained the momentum they had years ago. Consumers remain confused about what the brands stand for, in sharp contrast to the clearly focused images of competitors like Honda and Toyota.

7. The brand makes use of and coordinates a full repertoire of marketing activities to build equity. At its most basic level, a brand is made up of all the marketing elements that can be trademarked—logos, symbols, slogans, packaging, signage, and so on. Strong brands mix and match these elements to perform a number of brand-related functions, such as enhancing or reinforcing consumer awareness of the brand or its image and helping to protect the brand both competitively and legally.

Managers of the strongest brands also appreciate the specific roles that different marketing activities can play in building brand equity. They can, for example provide detailed product information. They can show consumers how and why a product is used, by whom, where, and when. They can associate a brand with a person, place, or thing to enhance or refine its image.

Some activities, such as traditional advertising, lend themselves best to "pull" functions—those meant to create consumer demand for a given product. Others, like trade promotions, work best as "push" programs—those designed to help push the product through distributors. When a brand makes good use of all its resources and also takes particular care to ensure that the essence of the brand is the same in all activities, it is hard to beat.

Coca-Cola is one of the best examples. The brand makes excellent use of many kinds of marketing activities. These include media advertising (such as the global "Always Coca-Cola" campaign); promotions (the recent effort focused on the return of the popular contour bottle, for example); and sponsorship (its extensive involvement with the Olympics). They also include direct response (the Coca-Cola catalog, which sells licensed Coke merchandise) and interactive media (the company's Web site, which offers, among other things, games, a trading post for collectors of Coke memorabilia, and a virtual look at the World of Coca-Cola museum in Atlanta). Through it all, the company always reinforces its key values of "originality," "classic refreshment," and so on. The brand is always the hero in Coca-Cola advertising.

8. The brand's managers understand what the brand means to consumers. Managers of strong brands appreciate the totality of their brand's image—that is, all the different perceptions, beliefs, attitudes, and behaviors customers associate with their brand, whether created intentionally by the company or not. As a result, managers are able to make decisions regarding the brand with confidence. If it's clear what customers like and don't like about a brand, and what core associations are linked to the brand, then it should also be clear whether any given action will dovetail nicely with the brand or create friction.

The Bic brand illustrates the kinds of problems that can arise when managers don't fully understand their brand's meaning. By emphasizing the convenience of inexpensive, disposable products, the French company Société Bic was able to create a market for nonrefillable ballpoint pens in the late 1950s, disposable cigarette lighters in the early 1970s, and disposable razors in the early 1980s. But in 1989, when Bic tried the same strategy with perfumes in the United States and Europe, the effort bombed.

The perfumes—two for women ("Nuit" and "Jour") and two for men ("Bic for Men" and "Bic Sport for Men")—were packaged in quarter-ounce glass spray bottles that looked like fat cigarette lighters and sold for about $5 each. They were displayed in plastic packages on racks at checkout counters throughout Bic's extensive distribution channels, which included 100,000 or so drugstores, supermarkets, and other mass merchandisers. At the time of the launch, a Bic spokesperson described the products as logical extensions of the Bic heritage: "High quality at affordable prices, convenient to purchase and convenient to use." The company spent $20 million on an advertising and promotion blitz that featured images of stylish people enjoying the perfumes and used the tag line "Paris in your pocket."

What went wrong? Although their other products did stand for convenience and for good quality at low prices, Bic's managers didn't understand that the overall brand image lacked a certain cachet with customers—a critical element when marketing something as tied to emotions as perfume. The marketers knew that customers understood the message they were sending with their earlier products. But they didn't have a handle on the associations that the customers had added to the brand image—a utilitarian, impersonal essence—which didn't at all lend itself to perfume.

By contrast, Gillette has been careful not to fall into the Bic trap. While all of its products benefit from a similarly extensive distribution system, it is very protective of the name carried by its razors, blades, and associated toiletries. The company's electric razors, for example, use the entirely separate Braun name, and its oral care products are marketed under the Oral B name.

9. The brand is given proper support, and that support is sustained over the long run. Brand equity must be carefully constructed. A firm foundation for brand equity requires that consumers have the proper depth and breadth of awareness and strong, favorable, and unique associations with the brand in their memory. Too often, managers want to take shortcuts and bypass more basic branding considerations—such as achieving the necessary level of brand awareness—in favor of concentrating on flashier aspects of brand building related to image.

A good example of lack of support comes from the oil and gas industry in the 1980s. In the late 1970s, consumers had an extremely positive image of Shell Oil and, according to market research, saw clear differences between that brand and its major competitors. In the early 1980s, however, for a variety of reasons, Shell cut back considerably on its advertising and marketing. Shell has yet to regain the ground it lost. The brand no longer enjoys the same special status in the eyes of consumers, who now view it as similar to other oil companies.

Another example is Coors Brewing. As Coors devoted increasing attention to growing the equity of its less-established brands like Coors Light, and introduced new products like Zima, ad support for the flagship beer plummeted from a peak of about $43 million in 1985 to just $4 million in 1993. What's more, the focus of the ads for Coors beer shifted from promoting an iconoclastic, independent, western image to reflecting more contemporary themes. Perhaps not surprisingly, sales of Coors beer dropped by half between 1989 and 1993. Finally in 1994, Coors began to address the problem, launching a campaign to prop up sales that returned to its original focus. Marketers at Coors admit that they did not consistently give the brand the attention it needed. As one commented: "We've not marketed Coors as aggressively as we should have in the past ten to 15 years."

Tapping customers' perceptions and beliefs often uncovers the true meaning of a brand.

10. The company monitors sources of brand equity. Strong brands generally make good and frequent use of in-depth brand audits and ongoing brand-tracking studies. A brand audit is an exercise designed to assess the health of a given brand. Typically, it consists of a detailed internal description of exactly how the brand has been marketed (called a "brand inventory") and a thorough external investigation, through focus groups and other consumer research, of exactly what the brand does and could mean to consumers (called a "brand exploratory"). Brand audits are particularly useful when they are scheduled on a periodic basis. It's critical for managers holding the reins of a brand portfolio to get a clear picture of the products and services being offered and how they are being marketed and branded. It's also important to see how that same picture looks to customers. Tapping customers' perceptions and beliefs often uncovers the true meaning of a brand, or group of brands, revealing where corporate and consumer views conflict and thus showing managers exactly where they have to refine or redirect their branding efforts or their marketing goals.

Tracking studies can build on brand audits by employing quantitative measures to provide current information about how a brand is performing for any given dimension. Generally, a tracking study will collect information on consumers' perceptions, attitudes, and behaviors on a routine basis over time; a thorough study can yield valuable tactical insights into the short-term effectiveness of marketing programs and activities. Whereas brand audits measure where the brand has been, tracking studies measure where the brand is now and whether marketing programs are having their intended effects.

The strongest brands, however, are also supported by formal brand-equity-management systems. Managers of these brands have a written document—a "brand equity charter"—that spells out the company's general philosophy with respect to brands and brand equity as concepts (what a brand is, why brands matter, why brand management is relevant to the company, and so on). It also summarizes the activities that make up brand audits, brand tracking, and other brand research; specifies the outcomes expected of them; and includes the latest findings gathered from such research. The charter then lays out guidelines for implementing brand strategies and tactics and documents proper treatment of the brand's trademark—the rules for how the logo can appear and be used on packaging, in ads, and so forth. These managers also assemble the results of their various tracking surveys and other relevant measures into a brand equity report, which is distributed to management on a monthly, quarterly, or annual basis. The brand equity report not only describes what is happening within a brand but also why.

Even a market leader can benefit by carefully monitoring its brand, as Disney aptly demonstrates. In the late 1980s, Disney became concerned that some of its characters (among them Mickey Mouse and Donald Duck) were being used inappropriately and becoming overexposed. To determine the severity of the problem, Disney undertook an extensive brand audit. First, as part of the brand inventory, managers compiled a list of all available Disney products (manufactured by the company and licensed) and all third-party promotions (complete with point-of-purchase displays and relevant merchandising) in stores worldwide. At the same time, as part of a brand exploratory, Disney launched its first major consumer research study to investigate how consumers felt about the Disney brand.

The results of the brand inventory were a revelation to senior managers. The Disney characters were on so many products and marketed in so many ways that it was difficult to understand how or why many of the decisions had been made in the first place. The consumer study only reinforced their concerns. The study indicated that people lumped all the product endorsements together. Disney was Disney to consumers, whether they saw the characters in films, or heard them in recordings, or associated them with theme parks or products.

Consequently, all products and services that used the Disney name or characters had an impact on Disney's brand equity. And because of the characters' broad exposure in the marketplace, many consumers had begun to feel that Disney was exploiting its name. Disney characters were used in a promotion of Johnson Wax, for instance, a product that would seemingly leverage almost nothing of value from the Disney name. Consumers were even upset when Disney characters were linked to well-regarded premium brands like Tide laundry detergent. In that case, consumers felt the characters added little value to the product. Worse yet, they were annoyed that the characters involved children in a purchasing decision that they otherwise would probably have ignored.

If consumers reacted so negatively to associating Disney with a strong brand like Tide, imagine how they reacted when they saw the hundreds of other Disney-licensed products and joint promotions. Disney's characters were hawking everything from diapers to cars to McDonald's hamburgers. Consumers reported that they resented all the endorsements because they felt they had a special, personal relationship with the characters and with Disney that should not be handled so carelessly.

As a result of the brand inventory and exploratory, Disney moved quickly to establish a brand equity team to better manage the brand franchise and more selectively evaluate licensing and other third-party promotional opportunities. One of the mandates of this team was to ensure that a consistent image for Disney—reinforcing its key association with fun family entertainment—was conveyed by all third-party products and services. Subsequently, Disney declined an offer to cobrand a mutual fund designed to help parents save for their children's college expenses. Although there was a family association, managers felt that a connection with the financial community suggested associations that were inconsistent with other aspects of the brand's image.

The Value of Balance

Building a strong brand involves maximizing all ten characteristics. And that is, clearly, a worthy goal. But in practice, it is tremendously difficult because in many cases when a company focuses on improving one, others may suffer.

Consider a premium brand facing a new market entrant with comparable features at a lower price. The brand's managers might be tempted to rethink their pricing strategy. Lowering prices might successfully block the new entrant from gaining market share in the short term. But what effect would that have in the long term? Will stepping outside its definition of "premium" change the brand in the minds of its target customers? Will it create the impression that the brand is no longer top of the line or that the innovation is no longer solid? Will the brand's message become cloudy? The price change may in fact attract customers from a different market segment to try the brand, producing a short-term blip in sales. But will those customers be the true target? Will their purchases put off the brand's original market?

The trick is to get a handle on how a brand performs on all ten attributes and then to evaluate any move from all possible perspectives. How will this new ad campaign affect customers' perception of price? How will this new product line affect the brand hierarchy in our portfolio? Does this tweak in positioning gain enough ground to offset any potential damage caused if customers feel we've been inconsistent?

One would think that monitoring brand performance wouldn't necessarily be included in the equation. But even effectively monitoring brand performance can have negative repercussions if you just go through the motions or don't follow through decisively on what you've learned.

Levi-Strauss's experiences are telling. In the mid-1990s, the company put together a comprehensive brand-equity-measurement system. Practically from the time the system was installed, it indicated that the brand image was beginning to slip, both in terms of the appeal of Levi's tight-fitting flagship 501 brand of jeans and how contemporary and cutting edge the overall Levi's brand was. The youth market was going for a much baggier look; competitors were rushing in to fill the gap. Distracted in part by an internal reengineering effort, however, Levi's was slow to respond and when it did, it came up with underfunded, transparently trendy ad campaigns that failed to resonate with its young target market. Its market share in the jeans category plummeted in the latter half of the 1990s. The result? Levi's has terminated its decades-long relationship with ad agency Foote, Cone & Belding and is now attempting to launch new products and new ad campaigns. For Levi's, putting in the system was not enough; perhaps if it had adhered more closely to other branding principles, concentrating on innovating and staying relevant to its customers, it could have better leveraged its market research data.

Negative examples and cautionary words abound, of course. But it is important to recognize that in strong brands the top ten traits have a positive, synergistic effect on one another; excelling at one characteristic makes it easier to excel at another. A deep understanding of a brand's meaning and a well-defined brand position, for example, guide development of an optimal marketing program. That, in turn, might lead to a more appropriate value-pricing strategy. Similarly, instituting an effective brand-equity-measurement system can help clarify a brand's meaning, capture consumers' reactions to pricing changes and other strategic shifts, and monitor the brand's ability to stay relevant to consumers through innovation.

Brand Equity as a Bridge

Ultimately, the power of a brand lies in the minds of consumers or customers, in what they have experienced and learned about the brand over time. Consumer knowledge is really at the heart of brand equity. This realization has important managerial implications.

In an abstract sense, brand equity provides marketers with a strategic bridge from their past to their future. That is, all the dollars spent each year on marketing can be thought of not so much as expenses but as investments—investments in what consumers know, feel, recall, believe, and think about the brand. And that knowledge dictates appropriate and inappropriate future directions for the brand—for it is consumers who will decide, based on their beliefs and attitudes about a given brand, where they think that brand should go and grant permission (or not) to any marketing tactic or program. If not properly designed and implemented, those expenditures may not be good investments—the right knowledge structures may not have been created in consumers' minds—but they are investments nonetheless.

Ultimately, the value to marketers of brand equity as a concept depends on how they use it. Brand equity can help marketers focus, giving them a way to interpret their past marketing performance and design their future marketing programs. Everything the company does can help enhance or detract from brand equity. Marketers who build strong brands have embraced the concept and use it to its fullest to clarify, implement, and communicate their marketing strategy.

Rating Your Brand

RATE YOUR BRAND on a scale of one to ten (one being extremely poor and ten being extremely good) for each characteristic below. Then create a bar chart that reflects the scores. Use the bar chart to generate discussion among all those individuals who participate in the management of your brands. Looking at the results in that manner should help you identify areas that need improvement, recognize areas in which you excel, and learn more about how your particular brand is configured.

It can also be helpful to create a report card and chart for competitors' brands simply by rating those brands based on your own perceptions, both as a competitor and as a consumer. As an outsider, you may know more about how their brands are received in the marketplace than they do.

Keep that in mind as you evaluate your own brand. Try to look at it through the eyes of consumers' rather than through your own knowledge of budgets, teams, and time spent on various initiatives.

The brand excels at delivering the benefits customers truly desire. Have you attempted to uncover unmet consumer needs and wants? By what methods? Do you focus relentlessly on maximizing your customers' product and service experiences? Do you have a system in place for getting comments from customers to the people who can effect change?

The brand stays relevant. Have you invested in product improvements that provide better value for your customers? Are you in touch with your customers' tastes? With the current market conditions? With new trends as they apply to your offering? Are your marketing decisions based on your knowledge of the above?

The pricing strategy is based on consumers' perceptions of value. Have you optimized price, cost, and quality to meet or exceed customers' expectations? Do you have a system in place to monitor customers' perceptions of your brand's value? Have you estimated how much value your customers believe the brand adds to your product?

The brand is properly positioned. Have you established necessary and competitive points of parity with competitors? Have you established desirable and deliverable points of difference?

The brand is consistent. Are you sure that your marketing programs are not sending conflicting messages and that they haven't done so over time? Conversely, are you adjusting your programs to keep current?

The brand portfolio and hierarchy make sense. Can the corporate brand create a seamless umbrella for all the brands in the portfolio? Do the brands in that portfolio hold individual niches? How extensively do the brands overlap? In what areas? Conversely, do the brands maximize market coverage? Do you have a brand hierarchy that is well thought out and well understood?

The brand makes use of and coordinates a full reportoire of marketing activities to build equity. Have you chosen or designed your brand name, logo, symbol, slogan, packaging, signage, and so forth to maximize brand awareness? Have you implemented integrated push and pull marketing activities that target both distributors and customers? Are you aware of all the marketing activities that involve your brand? Are the people managing each activity aware of one another? Have you capitalized on the unique capabilities of each communication option while ensuring that the meaning of the brand is consistently represented?

The brand's managers understand what the brand means to consumers. Do you know what customers like and don't like about a brand? Are you aware of all the core associations people make with your brand, whether intentionally created by your company or not? Have you created detailed, research-driven portraits of your target customers? Have you outlined customer-driven boundaries for brand extensions and guidelines for marketing programs?

The brand is given proper support, and that support is sustained over the long run. Are the successes or failures of marketing programs fully understood before they are changed? Is the brand given sufficient R&D support? Have you avoided the temptation to cut back marketing support for the brand in reaction to a downturn in the market or a slump in sales?

The company monitors sources of brand equity. Have you created a brand charter that defines the meaning and equity of the brand and how it should be treated? Do you conduct periodic brand audits to assess the health of your brand and to set strategic direction? Do you conduct routine tracking studies to evaluate current market performance? Do you regularly distribute brand equity reports that summarize all relevant research and information to assist marketers in making decisions? Have you assigned explicit responsibility for monitoring and preserving brand equity?

Originally published in January–February 2000
Reprint R00104

Bringing a Dying Brand Back to Life

MANNIE JACKSON

Executive Summary

IN 1992, THE HARLEM GLOBETROTTERS were headed toward extinction, but Honeywell executive and former Globetrotter Mannie Jackson believed the brand still had value after 75 years in the public eye. He bought the organization in order to translate this widespread brand recognition into financial results.

Jackson describes how he took over the Globetrotters in August 1993, intending to fold the team and replace it with an organization that would sell Globetrotters merchandise. But those plans changed when he met with the team for the first time and looked into the eyes of some of the great ones from the Globetrotters' past. Instead of shutting things down for good, Jackson started preaching to the squad about building a competitive team, about the team being well known for its contributions to charities, about the players working more with kids, and about rebuilding the quality of the organization. The players believed—and slowly but surely, audiences and arena managers did, too.

As Jackson got reacquainted with the organization, he found that the people who ran the company did not properly respect the players, the product, and the customers. To save the brand, Jackson put into practice three operating principles that had crystallized in his mind over the course of many years at Honeywell. First, the Globetrotters had to be reinvented in order to become relevant again; second, customers had to be shown that the company really cared about them; and third, an accountable organization had to be created. It wasn't easy, but by focusing on providing quality basketball, forging good business relationships, and insisting on accountability in the business, Jackson helped the Globetrotters dramatically increase revenue, profit, and attendance.

SOMETIMES IN BUSINESS, a good brand dies. Everyone knows and respects the brand, but there's a gap between people's knowledge and their desire to actually buy the product. When the company can't close that gap, the brand slowly but surely finds its way to the dustbin of history.

In 1992, the Harlem Globetrotters were heading down that path, but I thought I could get them back on the right road. I was convinced the brand still had value. So I talked things over with two bankers, who were also close friends of mine, and we got a group of investors together—mostly friends and business connections I'd made during my 25 years at Honeywell. We convinced them that the Globetrotters organization was worth buying. And over the years, we've been able to convert people's knowledge about the brand into a strong financial return. We've closed the gap and saved the Globetrotters brand.

When I took over the organization in August 1993, the games had an annual attendance of less than 300,000; this year we'll hit 2 million. In 1992, the company lost about $1 million on gross revenues of about $9 million; this year we'll have about $6 million in profit on gross revenues of about $60 million.

It hasn't been easy, of course. As I got reacquainted with the organization—I hadn't been involved with the Globetrotters since my playing days ended in the 1960s—I found that the people running the company did not respect the players or the product and were indifferent to the customers. The whole organization probably would have crashed and burned in another two years. To save the brand, I put into practice three operating principles that had crystallized in my mind over the course of many years at a major corporation; these principles form the core of my philosophy for running any business. First, the product had to be reinvented in order to become relevant again; second, customers had to be shown that we really cared about them; and third, an accountable organization had to be created—a real business. Before we get to that, though, you need to know a little bit more about the history of the team—and how I almost shut it down for good.

Changing Visions

The Globetrotters were founded in 1926 by Abe Saperstein, one of the greatest sports promoters who ever lived. He brought together eight African-American ballplayers, and they barnstormed the country, beating all comers. In an era of segregation, the team was probably the best in the world. That began to change in the 1950s, when the NBA integrated and started signing black players. But the Globetrotters continued to offer an entertaining mix of quality basketball, showmanship, and comedy.

The organization started to decline in the 1980s. The NBA was booming, and the Globetrotters were increasingly irrelevant as a competitive basketball team and stale as an entertainment choice. They were very poorly managed by the team's owner, International Broadcasting Company,

When I got interested in buying the organization, my first thought was that the team would go away. It had made a great contribution to the world, but it was over.

which also owned the Ice Capades and several amusement parks and theaters. By the early 1990s, IBC was in bankruptcy.

I was a senior vice president at Honeywell then, but I had a strong entrepreneurial streak that had pushed me to get involved as a silent owner-investor in other ventures. Although this kind of activity is unusual for a senior executive at a major company, I had the full blessing of Honeywell's CEO. As I considered buying the Globetrotters in 1992, I thought I could oversee the organization while staying with Honeywell, and in fact I did have a dual role until November 1994. By then, the organization's success combined with the enjoyment I was getting from being involved with it convinced me to leave Honeywell and run the Globetrotters full time.

When I got interested in buying the organization, my first thought was that the team would go away. It had run its course. Like another great African-American institution, the Negro baseball leagues, it had made a great contribution to the world, but it was over. I thought, if I can get the organization for a reasonable amount of money, I'll put together a museum, convince Hollywood to do a movie, write a book about the team's history, put licensed products in every neighborhood in the country, and make it cool to be identified with the team again.

The bankers rejected my first offer, which was to buy all of IBC, but they brought me in as a professional adviser to the Globetrotters. They figured I would be able to tell them exactly what to do with the organization so they could get the maximum value when they eventually sold it.

I met with the team for the first time in Boston in March 1992, and I gave a speech to the group. I had intended to tell them that we would be folding the team, but as I got into the speech and looked into the eyes of some of the great ones from the team's past, I started telling a different story. You know how sometimes ideas just come through you, and you start talking without a script? That's what happened to me. I started talking about building a competitive team, being known for our contributions to charity, being good to kids, and rebuilding the quality of the organization. Suddenly I wasn't the same guy who had written a business plan in his mind in which the team folded and was replaced by a licensed-product organization.

The players got excited; they believed in me. "Saving the Globetrotters has got to be a religion for us," I told them. "You guys are my disciples; I'm going to be your leader. If you don't want to join me, get out of here now." No one left, and when I finished speaking, I knew they were with me. I went back to my hotel room and wrote down everything I'd said.

Now I was excited, too, but I knew that I needed to test and expand my vision. I put together a list of about 12 people I respected—high-level marketing people from Honeywell, former Globetrotters, an arena owner—and I brought them together for three and a half days at a farm I rented in southern Minnesota. I'd come to know these people through my business ties over the years, and they attended the off-site meeting out of friendship and an interest in the fate of the organization. We started dreaming and asking ourselves, What could the Globetrotters be? What should they be? We met from morning till midnight each day, and I was able to build a detailed strategic plan from those meetings.

After this summit, I went back to the bankers who owned the team at that point, and I told them I'd give them $5.5 million for the Globetrotters alone. They were getting concerned—another season was rolling around, and they wanted to move. Compared with other bidders, I had the best story about the organization's future, so they agreed to sell a majority interest to me. I now had to make the story real, and the first step was turning the product into something that people would care about again.

Reinventing the Product

By 1993, the Globetrotters were simply not relevant. They weren't stylish, and they weren't cool. They weren't a priority for anyone—they weren't on MTV or *The Tonight Show*, and the president didn't invite them to the White House. I wanted to find out how bad the damage was, so we held a series of focus groups around the country and brought together people who had seen us perform with those who hadn't. The meetings were very expensive and difficult to set up, but the information we got as a result was more than worth it. Young people would tell us they didn't know anything about the Globetrotters, and many of the older folks hadn't heard about us recently. "How good are you really?" they would ask. "Are you just clowns, or can you play basketball?"

I decided we could become relevant if what we put on the basketball floor each night was top quality. We have two different ways of showing what we can do. About 30 or 40 times a year, we bring together our best players to compete against first-rate teams all over the world. For example, last fall we played both Purdue and Michigan State, the NCAA champion. We beat Purdue and played Michigan State close. Games like that make it impossible for people to say that our guys can't hold their own against top-notch basketball teams.

When we are not playing competitive games, our three touring teams play against three exhibition teams. Our philosophy is simple. In each game, we set out to do three things: we're going to show you we can play basketball, we're going to give an exhibition of basketball feats you've never seen live before, and we're going to make you laugh and feel good.

In each exhibition game, we start off playing serious, competitive basketball, and the fans in the audience quickly realize that our guys can really play. They'll recognize players who were at Maryland or UCLA or Kentucky. Then we move on to the highlight-film part of the game. We have players who do things you can only see if you come to one of our events, like shooting behind-the-back hook shots or dunking through a 12-foot basket, which is the world record. We stress perfect execution every single night so people will say, "Wow, I've never seen anything like that before." The third part of each game is the stand-up comedy. We have one or two guys on each team who are world-class comics. They can walk into an arena full of 20,000 people and get everyone laughing and feeling better about the world.

The whole package is choreographed like a Broadway musical. Let's face it, a two-hour basketball game can be pretty dull. To get rid of the dead time, we carefully added music to our events. Our announcers now have a computer board, and they plug in tracks that fit with what's happening on the floor. So if the action is fast paced, they might play a hip-hop song, and if the other team is coming back, they might play a big-band dance tune. And then, when the comics come on, everything stops. They go out into the audience with body microphones, tell jokes, do comedy routines. Sometimes it's completely outrageous, but it's always appropriate for families.

I learned an important lesson about the product several years ago when I brought an executive from Disney, one of our sponsors, to a game in Europe. As we watched, I asked him what he would do different. He sat for a while and then he said, "You know what? It's a 90-minute show, no more." I was shocked. We had been stretching out the events for two and a half hours, like NBA games. On school nights, kids would be falling asleep. Now we do it all in 90 fast-paced minutes, and people are happy when they leave.

We're cool but not hip-hop cool, and we never will be. Our brand means being family friendly, so we keep ticket prices relatively low, and we make sure our players sign autographs, talk to kids, and engage with the fans in the stands. We don't do anything that would embarrass a mom and dad who've brought their kids to a game.

Many people still don't believe that our guys play top-level basketball. That's something we have to work on

continually. But the 2 million people who see us every
year know the truth, and they leave our events having
seen both great basketball and great entertainment.

Putting Customers at the Center

Having a terrific product is not always enough to sustain
a brand. The essence of the Globetrotters business is promotions and relationships—with the media, with sponsors, and especially with customers. Our first line of customers is the people who own the arenas and their
marketing staffs. If they won't book your event and promote it, you're in big trouble—you won't even get to the
next line of customers, the people who actually buy the
tickets.

I believed that good relationships with the media and
the arenas would lead to strong event promotion. To create those relationships, I leveraged my business identity
with the *Wall Street Journal* and with anyone from the
business side of other publications who would listen to
an African-American executive who had worked for
many years at Honeywell talk about branding and
turnaround strategies. I had to get enough credibility in
the business community so that when I walked into the
office of General Mills or Denny's or Target or Reebok,
the executives there would see me first as a capable busi-
nessperson. I gave them the same brand reinvention
story that I had given to the players, and I gave it over
and over again. I created a buzz that helped me get both
sponsorship dollars and the immediate attention and
respect of the arena owners and their staffs.

The Globetrotters was just one event out of 200 a year
for the arena people, and if the show hadn't done well the
year before, their instinct was to skip promoting us this

year, or maybe even just to drop us from the schedule. That's why one of the first things I did was to cut the advertising budget in half and use that money to hire regional marketing people. The marketers are assigned to 50 cities, and all they do year round is meet with the arena managers, their marketing staffs, and with businesses that want to promote our events. They work with the arenas to develop a promotions strategy for each game to make sure it's successful. And the relationships we've forged with the people in the arenas have paid off in the way we get promoted. The arena managers have friends who sponsor events. They also have contacts who do group sales, and they have relationships with the local media. Access to these channels has been invaluable.

Media attention helps cement our relationships with fans and increases the promotion of our events. I read somewhere 20 years ago that if you hit people with three events in quick succession, they'll remember you. So we come up with three major events twice a year that go bang, bang, bang—a series of games against college stars, the players meeting with the pope or Nelson Mandela, our 75th anniversary celebration at the United Center in Chicago, and so on. These events keep the Globetrotters in front of the public, and the publicity we get from them is more than worth the costs we bear in arranging them.

We use each event to connect directly with fans, the customers who buy from our sponsors and fill the arenas, and we also reach out to our audience in other ways. Our social commitment, an important part of the brand's value, is at the heart of this. We put on 25 or 30 summer camps every year to connect with young fans. They're sponsored by one of our partners, Denny's, and we make a special point of helping disadvantaged kids. Many of them aren't required to pay anything to attend. In addition, our regional marketing people identify the leading charity in the cities we visit. We'll get in touch with that group and say, "We're coming to town, what can we do for you?" For example, I might donate my time and speak at a fund-raising dinner at an organization's annual meeting. To get closer to people, our players visit hospitals, schools, and youth clubs year round.

Like any company engaged in grassroots marketing, we've had to overcome obstacles. My efforts to get sponsors have been very frustrating at times. I would make it plain to marketing executives why sponsoring the Globetrotters would be a good business decision, but too many people basically said to me, "Don't confuse me with facts." A lot of what goes on involving sponsorships is really irrational. It's like deciding whether to buy a corporate jet. You can draw up a list of pros and cons, but ultimately it comes down to one question: do you want the jet or not? The same is true, unfortunately, for the way too many decisions about sponsorships get made.

Some companies, though, have been great for us. Our relationship with Disney has worked out very well. It all started when the president of Disney's Wide World of Sports got in touch with me through mutual friends. We met and arranged to play ten to 15 games a year at their facility in Orlando, and we have our annual training camp there. The financial

I disrupted the status quo and created a new language around the business. Many of the organization's old-timers had to leave. They couldn't adapt.

arrangement has been good, and there's a halo effect that comes from being in the relationship. When commercial partners or others hear that we're aligned with Disney, it locks us into their minds as family entertainment. And I can take that result to our players and staff and say, "You see, this is what I mean when I talk about the importance of brand identity." When it is developed in the right way, it can be a very powerful tool.

Running the Brand Like a Business

In 1993, the organization was in bad shape. The infrastructure was fragile, and some of the attitudes were incredibly unprofessional. I came in and demanded that we run a responsible, profitable business. I disrupted the status quo and created a new language around the business. Many of the organization's old-timers had to leave. They just couldn't adapt.

I had to start from square one with the staff on how to run the business responsibly. While I was still with Honeywell, I'd fly out to various Globetrotters' offices on Friday nights and meet with people on Saturdays and Sundays. I remember one day I said in a meeting, "We are going to play in the UK and from there we're going to spread across Europe. I would like you to develop a pan-European strategy that covers an investment period in year one and shows positive results in years two, three, and four." I talked for over an hour on that subject and then went home to Minneapolis. Monday morning, my phone rang at the Honeywell office, and it was my vice president of marketing for the Globetrotters. She said, "Do you mind if I ask you a question? What's a strategy?" So I went back the next week and started teaching classes on these very basic points.

My years at Honeywell had taught me that all roads lead to numbers. (For more on what I learned at Honeywell, see "The Building Blocks of Experience" at the end of this article.) You learn a lot about the character of an organization when you look at its finances. I knew there were leaks, that we were overpaying consultants and lawyers, that people weren't keeping a close eye on the numbers. I started holding everyone accountable.

It wasn't hard to be away from the Globetrotters for four or five days during those first months, because I used a formula I had learned from Lee Iacocca. On Saturday, I gave people three things to do during the next week, and I gave out pens emblazoned with the motto "We do what we say we're going to do." Everyone had a pen, but if someone didn't come through, I took it away from them. That first time it was just a friendly warning, but I didn't allow a lot of mistakes.

I set up a procedure in which every game or event had a forecast for cost, revenue, and operating profit. I wanted to be called every night before midnight with the reconciliation, and I wanted a faxed copy as well. My computer and my fax machine were jumping off the table. Cash-flow reports were coming in all the time.

We started running the Globetrotters on the basis of gross-profit and break-even analyses. That's the language around here now: what's the break-even on this event? And cash and gross profit are a religion for us, just as they were at Honeywell. You really have to work to keep track of all the nickels and to make sure every one of your managers with budget responsibility is held accountable—but you know where the business stands all the time when you do these analyses.

I expect people in the organization sometimes to get tired of me, even mad at me, but no one is ever allowed to get mad at the brand.

We also broke up the company into business units. We were shocked by what we found. We had several loss leaders. We weren't investing in some parts of the business that were bringing in big profits. Strong business units were subsidizing weak ones. Breaking up the business allowed us to run the units according to return on capital, and we assigned staff champions and set profitability hurdles for each one.

One unit that has cleared its hurdles with a lot of room to spare is the merchandising business. We didn't actually own the business until 1998, when we bought the inventory for less than $200,000. The company that owned it had been giving us up to $800,000 a year, which we thought was great—no one had ever looked closely at what they were doing over there, and it was like they were giving us free money. Now we earn more than $3 million in revenue per year from the business, and half of that is profit. The cash has been great, and we've been able to get closer to the customer by having our own people run this business.

Finally, the success of the brand as a business comes down to a fundamental point. I expect people in the organization sometimes to get tired of me, even mad at me, but no one is ever allowed to get mad at the brand. They like what the brand is, and they can define it. It guides everything we do. The brand has taken on a life that's bigger than all of us. As the organization's leader, I think of myself as the chief brand cop and spokesman, and I enjoy every minute of it.

When I took over, the Globetrotters were on life support. Now, thanks to the way we've implemented the three principles, the brand is much healthier. We can't afford to be complacent, however. There's still a big gap between how many people know us and the financial results we get from that recognition. Closing that gap is a real challenge, and we're keenly aware that great brands can go out of business. Nobody's safe these days.

I've been very fortunate to have a great team around me. As the business prospered, I was able to buy out all but three of my original partners, and their investments paid off very well for them. It wasn't part of my original plan to still be running this business, but the improvements to the product that we've made, the financial success we've enjoyed, and the good we do with our charitable initiatives keep me focused and energized. I could be home taking it easy or playing golf, but I want to be here because I love basketball and the game of business.

The Building Blocks of Experience

I LEARNED A LOT DURING my 25 years at Honeywell that I was able to use to save the Globetrotters brand. My primary teacher was Ed Spencer, the company's CEO from 1979 to 1987. He taught me the following important lessons:

- **Create a culture of accountability.** Ed didn't just hold people accountable, he created a culture of accountability that everyone at Honeywell understood. When you hit a sales target, he threw a party for you, and morale at the company was very high as a result. I do the same thing. Every year that we hit or exceed our targets, I take the entire company on a three-day trip to celebrate and reflect on our accomplishments.

- **Think about how you are using your time.** Ed planted one question in the forefront of my mind: is what you are doing the best use of your time and of corporate resources? I've taught the Globetrotters staff to think the same way, and it really makes people more efficient overnight.

- **Don't be satisfied with last year's results.** Ed raised the standards and the expectations every year. I'm the same way. We have a bar chart that hangs on the wall, and we define success as bringing the bar to a higher level. To remind us of how far we've come, the chart starts with our dismal numbers from 1993.

- **See people for what they can become.** Ed was a master of choosing odd people to do jobs. He saw people for their potential, not just for what was on their résumés. At the Globetrotters, I made a 20-year-old the president of our merchandising unit, and I put a guy who was the trainer for the basketball team into the position of executive vice president for marketing—and they're both doing an outstanding job.

- **Pretend I'm in the room.** When I was doing mergers and acquisitions for Honeywell, I once asked Ed how he could trust me not to make mistakes in judgment with such big transactions. He said, "Just assume I'm in the room with you. If a deal doesn't feel right—if you wouldn't do it with me sitting next to you—walk away." I tell my players the same thing: "If you're in a club where things are getting out of hand—or in any other situation that could lead to trouble—assume I'm there watching your behavior. If it doesn't feel right, just walk away from it."

There is one thing that I didn't get from Ed or from Honeywell that's important to mention: mental and physical stamina. I was fortunate to be born with the physiology that has allowed me to put in long hours. For anyone trying to lead a company, regardless of its size, that's a very valuable capacity.

Originally published in May 2001
Reprint R0105B

How to Fight a Price War

AKSHAY R. RAO, MARK E. BERGEN,
AND SCOTT DAVIS

Executive Summary

PRICE WARS ARE A FACT OF LIFE, whether we're talking about the fast-paced world of knowledge products,
the marketing of Internet appliances, or the staid, traditional sales of aluminum castings. If you're a manager
and you're not in battle currently, you probably will be
soon, so it's never too early to prepare.

The authors describe the causes and characteristics
of price wars and explain how companies can fight
them, flee them—or even start them. The authors say the
best defense in a pricing battle isn't to simply match price
cut for price cut; they emphasize other options for protecting market share.

For instance, companies can compete on quality
instead of price; they can alert customers to the risks and
negative consequences of choosing a low-priced option.
Companies can reveal their strategic intentions and

capabilities; just the threat of a major price action might hold rivals' pricing moves in check. And, finally, companies can seek support from interested third parties—governments, customers, and vendors, for instance—to help avert a price war.

If a company chooses to compete on price, the authors suggest using complex pricing actions, cutting prices in certain channels, or introducing new products or flanking brands—each of which lets companies selectively target only those segments of the market that are under competitive threat. A simple tit-for-tat price move should be the last resort—and managers should act swiftly and decisively so competitors will know that any revenue gains will be short-lived.

In the battle to capture the customer, companies use a wide range of tactics to ward off competitors. Increasingly, price is the weapon of choice—and frequently the skirmishing degenerates into a price war.

Creating low-price appeal is often the goal, but the result of one retaliatory price slashing after another is often a precipitous decline in industry profits. Look at the airline price wars of 1992. When American Airlines, Northwest Airlines, and other U.S. carriers went toe-to-toe in matching and exceeding one another's reduced fares, the result was record volumes of air travel—and record losses. Some estimates suggest that the overall losses suffered by the industry that year exceed the combined profits for the entire industry from its inception.

Price wars can create economically devastating and psychologically debilitating situations that take an extraordinary toll on an individual, a company, and industry profitability. No matter who wins, the combatants all seem to end up worse off than before they joined the battle. And yet, price wars are becoming increasingly common and uncommonly fierce. Consider the following two examples:

- In July 1999, Sprint announced a nighttime long-distance rate of 5 cents per minute. In August 1999, MCI matched Sprint's off-peak rate. Later that month, AT&T acknowledged that revenue from its consumer long-distance business was falling, and the company cut its long-distance rates to 7 cents per minute all day, everyday, for a monthly fee of $5.95. AT&T's stock dropped 4.7% the day of the announcement. MCI's stock price dropped 2.5%; Sprint's fell 3.8%.

- E-Trade and other electronic brokers are changing the competitive terrain of financial services with their extraordinarily low-priced brokerage services. The prevailing price for discount trades has fallen from $30 to $15 to $8 in the past few years.

There is little doubt, in the first example, that the major players in the long-distance phone business are in a price war. Price reductions, per-second billing, and free calls are the principal weapons the players bring to the competitive arena. There is little talk from any of the carriers about service, quality, brand equity, and other non-price factors that might add value to a product or service. Virtually every competitive move is based on price, and every countermeasure is a retaliatory price cut.

In the second example, the competitive situation is subtly different—and yet still very much a price war. E-Trade's success demonstrates how the emergence of the Internet has fundamentally changed the cost of doing business. Consequently, even businesses such as Charles Schwab, which used to compete primarily on low-price appeal, are chanting a "quality" mantra. Meanwhile, Merrill Lynch and American Express have recognized that the emergence of the Internet will affect pricing and are changing their price structures to include free on-line trades

Price wars are becoming more common because managers tend to view a price change as an easy, quick, and reversible action.

for high-end customers. These companies appear to be engaged in more focused pricing battles, unlike the "globalized" price war in the long-distance phone market.

Most managers will be involved in a price war at some point in their careers. Every price cut is potentially the first salvo, and some discounts routinely lead to retaliatory price cuts that then escalate into a full-blown price war. That's why it's a good idea to consider other options before starting a price war or responding to an aggressive price move with a retaliatory one. Often, companies can avoid a debilitating price war altogether by using a set of alternative tactics. Our goal is to describe an arsenal of weapons other than price cuts that managers who are engaged in or contemplating a price war may also want to consider. (See "Ways to Fight a Price War" for examples.)

Take Inventory

Generally, price wars start because somebody somewhere thinks prices in a certain market are too high. Or someone is willing to buy market share at the expense of current margins. Price wars are becoming more common because managers tend to view a price change as an easy, quick, and reversible action. When businesses don't trust or know one another very well, the pricing battles can escalate very quickly. And whether they play out in the physical or the virtual world, price wars have a similar set of antecedents. By understanding their causes and characteristics, managers can make sensible decisions about when and how to fight a price war, when to flee one—and even when to start one.

Ways to Fight a Price War

Tactic	Example
Nonprice Responses	
Reveal your strategic intentions and capabilities	Offer to match competitors' prices, offer everyday low pricing, or reveal your cost advantage.
Compete on quality	Increase product differentiation by adding features to a product, or build awareness of existing features and their benefits. Emphasize the performance risks in low-priced options.
Co-opt contributors	Form strategic partnerships by offering cooperative or exclusive deals with suppliers, resellers, or providers of related services.
Price Responses	
Use complex price actions	Offer bundled prices, two-part pricing, quantity discounts, price promotions, or loyalty programs for products.
Introduce new products	Introduce flanking brands that compete in customer segments that are being challenged by competitors.
Deploy simple price actions	Adjust the product's regular price in response to a competitor's price change or another potential entry into the market.

The first step, then, is diagnosis. Consider a small commodities supplier that suddenly found that its largest competitor had slashed prices to a level well below the small company's costs. One option the smaller company considered was to lower its price in a tit-for-tat move. But that price would have been below the supplier's marginal cost; it would have suffered debilitating losses. Fortunately, a few phone calls revealed that its adversary was attempting to drive the supplier out of the local market by underpricing its products locally but maintaining high prices elsewhere. The supplier correctly diagnosed the pricing move as predatory and elected to do two things. First, the manager called customers in the competitor's home market to let them know that the price-cutter was offering special deals in another market. Second, he called local customers and asked them for their support, pointing out that if the smaller supplier was driven off the market, its customers would be facing a monopolist. The short-term price cuts would turn into long-term price hikes. The supplier identified solutions that eschewed further price cuts and thus averted a price war.

Intelligent analysis that leads to accurate diagnosis is more than half the cure. The process emphasizes understanding the opportunities for pricing actions based on current market trends and responding to competitors' actions based on the players and their resources. Not only is it necessary to understand why a price war is occurring or may occur, it also is critical to recognize where to look for the resources to do battle.

Good diagnoses involve analyzing four key areas in the theater of operations. They are *customer issues* such as price sensitivity and the customer segments that may emerge if prices change; *company issues* such as a business's cost structures, capabilities, and strategic position-ing; *competitor issues,* such as a rival's cost structures, capabilities, and strategic positioning; and *contributor issues,* or the other players in the industry whose self-interest or profiles may affect the outcome of a price war. (For a more detailed explanation of such analyses, see "Analyzing the Battleground" at the end of this article.)

Companies that step back and examine those four areas carefully often find that they actually have quite a few different options—including defusing the conflict, fighting it out on several fronts, or retreating. We'll look at some of those strategies and how companies have deployed them successfully.

Stop the War Before It Starts

There are several ways to stop a price war before it starts. One is to make sure your competitors understand the rationale behind your pricing policies. In other words, *reveal your strategic intentions.* Price-matching policies, everyday low pricing, and other public statements may communicate to competitors that you intend to fight a price war using all possible resources. But frequently these declarations about low prices, or about not engag-ing in price promotions, aren't low-price strategies at all. Such announcements are simply a way to tell competi-tors that you prefer to compete on dimensions other than price. When your competitors agree that such com-petition will be more profitable than competing on price, they'll tend to go along. That is precisely what happened when Winn-Dixie followed the Big Star supermarket chain in North Carolina and announced that it, too, would meet or beat mutual rival Food Lion's prices. After two years, the number of equipriced products among 79 commonly purchased brand items at the supermarkets had more than doubled. Further, the overall market price level had increased for these products. What happened? The stores stopped competing on price. In fact, the data suggest that Food Lion raised its prices after its competitors announced they would match Food Lion's prices.

Making sure that your competitors know that your costs are low is another option—one that effectively warns them about the potential consequences of a price war. Hence it sometimes pays to *reveal your cost advantage.* Sara Lee has low variable costs, yet its products are relatively high priced compared with those of competitors. In the event of a price war, Sara Lee can drop its prices to levels that its competitors can't profitably match. The common knowledge about this low cost deters price cutting from competitors.

Sara Lee's management realizes that price cuts would be inconsistent with its strategic position of brand differentiation. Rather than use its low-cost structure to compete on price to build market share, Sara Lee uses its low costs as an implicit threat that helps prevent price wars. Essentially, a business that has relatively low variable costs enjoys an enviable advantage in a price war since competitors cannot sustain a price below their own variable costs in the long run. But low-cost companies should carefully consider their strategic positions before they start or join a price war. Lower costs often tempt a business to cut its prices, but doing so can diminish consumers' perceptions of quality and may trigger an unprofitable price war.

Responding with Nonprice Actions

Sometimes an analysis of the market reveals that several customer segments exhibit different degrees of sensitivity to price and quality. (See "Price Sensitivity on the Web" at the end of this article for a look at how managers can identify and exploit differences in customers' price sensitivities—even in an information-rich environment.) Understanding the basis for certain customers' price sensitivities lets managers creatively respond to a rival's price cut without cutting their own prices. For example, a company might be able to *focus on quality, not price.*

Southeast Asia went through a rough time in 1997, particularly in the luxury product and service areas. The region's economy was unstable, Indonesian forest fires were wreaking havoc with the smog index, and tourism was clearly suffering. The economic turmoil dramatically reduced the value of the Malaysian ringgit to about half its value a few years earlier. The cost of a hotel room plummeted along with the nose-diving currency, yet hotel rooms went a-begging. What did the luxury hotel operators do to attract customers? They dropped their room rates even further. Luxury hotels in Malaysia entered a price war. All but one.

The Ritz-Carlton chose to steer clear of the fray. Instead, James McBride, the hotel's general manager, became creative. He greeted arriving flights with music, mimosas, discount coupons, and a model room. Passengers with reservations at other hotels began to defect to the Ritz at alarming rates. McBride provided his cellular phone number in newspaper ads so people could call him directly for reservations. Guests had round-the-clock access to a "technology butler" who could fix laptops and other electronic devices. The Ritz offered a "bath menu" of drinks and snacks to be served along with butler-drawn baths. Guests who stayed more than five nights received an embroidered pillowcase.

When luxury hotels start cutting their guest rates, their ability to offer "luxury" accoutrements drops. That means no fresh flowers, fewer towels, and a noticeable shortage of staff. But the Ritz kept its rates above 200 ringgit (about $52 U.S.) and was able to pay for low-cost services such as providing the embroidered pillow-cases. Most important, the Ritz avoided any damage to its brand equity, something that could have easily occurred if typical Ritz customers arrived at the hotel and found it filled with noisy

One way companies can avoid a price war is to alert customers to risk—specifically, the risk of poor product quality. A related weapon is to emphasize other negative consequences.

backpacking tourists or large families, all taking advantage of low prices. The negative spillover onto other Ritz properties could have been significant.

The Ritz-Carlton Kuala Lumpur last fall had no more empty rooms than its competitors; in fact, occupancy rates were up to 60% compared with a 50% occupancy rate in 1998. Perhaps most important, monthly gross operating profit on revenue of 2.2 million ringgit is about 400,000 ringgit—a return of about 18%.

Another way companies can avoid a price war is to *alert customers to risk*—specifically, the risk of poor quality. A senior product manager from the European operation of a large multinational pharmaceutical corporation lamented her recent pricing predicament. Her company's product, a medical diagnostic device, was the market-share leader, but a rival company had recently become aggressive on price. "They're crazy! Don't they see what they're doing to profits in the industry? Nobody can make money at these prices. What should I do? I've tried everything, and I can't get them to see the error of their ways," she said.

Not surprisingly, research confirmed that a large segment of customers in this "life and death" industry—doctors and testing laboratories—was quite risk averse and sensitive to variations in a product's performance. So rather than compete on price, the multinational appealed to customers' concerns about performance by emphasizing product enhancements such as improved reliability and greater detail in the information generated by the diagnostic device and by alerting buyers to the negative consequences of incomplete diagnoses. Some sales were lost to lower-priced products from the competitor, but the quality-sensitive segment allowed the multinational to maintain reasonable margins and avoid the negative spiral of a price war.

Federal Express provides another good example of how a company can appeal to performance sensitivity among customers. FedEx's brand equity exceeds that of virtually any company in the package delivery business. The shipping giant has built an enviable level of consumer recall and recognition through a highly effective advertising campaign. By emphasizing in ads and through other marketing efforts that a customer's package will "absolutely, positively" be there on time, FedEx plays on customers' risk aversion when dealing with time-sensitive documents.

A related weapon that companies can use to avert or battle a price war is to *emphasize other negative consequences.* The NutraSweet company employed this strategy when it faced the expiration of its patent. The company feared considerable price pressure from the producers of aspartame, the generic version of NutraSweet. A worst-case scenario would involve one of NutraSweet's major customers, such as Coca-Cola or Pepsi, switching to aspartame. If one of the companies switched, NutraSweet's contingency plan—which it shared with wavering Coke and Pepsi executives in Atlanta and New York—was a week-long advertising blitz that would alert consumers that "the other cola" was the only one that contained NutraSweet. Given the size of the market for carbonated soft drinks, NutraSweet's brand equity in the diet-conscious segment, and the potential short-term loss in market share and profits, this threat had teeth. NutraSweet successfully played one customer against another, emphasizing dire and unpalatable consequences, and thus averted a debilitating price war.

A final nonprice option involves *seeking help,* or appealing to contributors to weigh in on the competitive situation. For instance, when Sony entered the market for high-end imaging systems, the leaders in the imaging systems market in Belgium appealed to and received help from the central Belgian government. Not all companies can count on the government to come to their aid, of course. So companies might appeal to customers, vendors, channel partners, independent sales representatives, and other like-minded players if the price war could mean the company's demise. For instance, in the 1990s, Northwest Airlines appealed to its labor unions and received dramatic wage concessions so it could compete on price in a tight air-travel market.

Managers can localize a price war to a limited theater of operation—and cut down the opportunities for the war to spill into other markets.

Using Selective Pricing Actions

Employing complex options such as multiple-part pricing, quantity discounts, time-of-use pricing, bundling, and so on lets price warriors selectively cut rates for only those segments of the population that are under competitive threat.

One common—and classic—tactic is to *change customers' choices,* or reframe the price war in the minds of customers. McDonald's did it successfully when it faced Taco Bell's 59-cent taco strategy in the 1980s. By bundling burgers, fries, and drinks into "value meals," McDonald's reframed the price war from "tacos versus burgers" to "lunch versus lunch." Similarly, smart managers use quantity discounts or loyalty programs to insulate themselves from a price war. They avoid across-the-board price cuts, and they limit price reductions to areas in which they are vulnerable. In this way, managers can localize a price war to a limited theater of operation—and cut down the opportunities for the war to spill into other markets.

Therefore, another selective-pricing tactic might be to *modify only certain prices.* For instance, Sun Country Airlines, a discount carrier, entered Northwest's Minneapolis–St. Paul hub with 16 planes providing service to 14 cities. Sun Country's round-trip airfare to any location was generally low: Minneapolis to Boston was roughly $308. Rather than engage in a systemwide price cut, Northwest retained its existing fare structure with minor modifications. A Minneapolis–Boston round-trip was a relatively low $310 if tickets were purchased seven days in advance—but only for a flight that departed at 7:10 AM and returned at 11:10 AM. Curiously enough, Sun Country's only flight on that route departed Minneapolis at 7 AM and Boston at 11:20 AM. Northwest also employed several other resources, such as travel agents, to fend off Sun Country. Northwest reasoned that Sun Country did not have the infrastructure necessary to engage in an all-out price war and chose to not engage in any preemptive price cutting at times other than the flights directly affected. By targeting only certain fares for discounts, Northwest minimized internal changes but could still counter Sun Country's pricing ploy.

On another selective-pricing front, companies may use a *fighting brand.* In the early 1990s, Kao Corporation entered the diskette market with a low-priced product. Rather than drop its prices, 3M launched a flanking brand of low-priced diskettes called Highland because it knew that a large group of its customers was loyal to the 3M brand. Simply dropping the price on the 3M brand might have diluted 3M's quality image and its profits and may have stimulated further price cuts by Kao.

Because it understood its customers, 3M knew that many different segments of price-sensitive customers existed. Some people buy cheap diskettes, and some people don't care how much they pay for diskettes. More important, some people think cheap diskettes are probably of poor quality, and they may not buy them if the price is too low—perhaps because they are terrified of losing their data. 3M avoided the trap of charging what the market will bear. It recognized that markets will bear many prices, some better than others. That insight underpins the strategies of many software companies. For instance, marginally different versions of the same voice-recognition software can range in price from $79 to $8,000 depending on who the buyer is.[1]

You may not need a new brand to counter a price cut, just a new package. Consider the case of a major consumer-products company that faced an aggressive price-cutting competitor. The defending company finally dropped the price of its economy-size product with a "buy one, get one free" offer. Since the economy-size product lasts six months, the company took high-volume, price-sensitive users off the market for nearly a year. The resulting low sales of the competitor's product convinced the rival to cease and desist.

That illustration has several instructive elements to it. First, an acute understanding of the competitor's abilities, motives, and mind-set allowed the defending company to react effectively to a price war. Second, the expertise was complemented with a clear understanding of consumer behavior that allowed the company to prevent a price war. Third, the new entrant clearly picked the wrong adversary. The defending company was willing to suffer some losses (through cannibalization) in order to protect its turf.

Companies may also opt to *cut prices in certain channels.* Perhaps the single largest driver of price cuts and resulting price wars is excess capacity. The temptation to revive idle plants by stimulating demand through lower prices is often irresistible. But smart managers consider other options first. For instance, companies in the packaged-goods industry frequently sell off-brand or private-label versions of their national brands at low prices, ensuring that any price wars won't damage the brand equity of the national brands.

Similarly, airlines such as Delta are making a dent in reducing their unsold inventory by offering seats to consolidators and auction houses such as Priceline.com and Cheaptickets.com. The airlines are selling tickets to price-sensitive customers who don't care about flight times, number of stops, or frequent-flyer miles. Because the customer's point of contact is with the consolidator and not with the airline, the airline's image is protected—in much the same way that a nationally branded soup manufacturer protects its image by selling excess capacity under a private label.

But engaging in "stealth marketing" by selling low-priced, functionally equivalent alternatives through unrelated brand names or in foreign markets may still trigger price wars. If consumers recognize that the quality of the private-label product is comparable to that of the branded option, then the price of the branded option will need to drop. In many cases, it is best to leave plant capacity idle, since the attempt to revive it may trigger margin-destroying price competition. In fact, the idle capacity can be used as a weapon; a company then wields the credible threat of being able to flood the market with cheaper products should a competitor start cutting its prices.

Fight It Out

Although we feel strongly that direct, retaliatory price cuts should be a last resort, we do recognize that it is sometimes simply impossible to avoid a price war. Consider the case of personal computers. Expansion in this industry is occurring primarily at the low end as more and more price-sensitive consumers enter the market for PCs. EMachines, in Irvine, California, sells PCs that feature Intel's Celeron processor (a 366 MHz chip), a 4.3 gigabyte hard drive, and a host of other functions for roughly $400. High-profile brands such as HP and IBM are being forced to consider pricing their PCs in the $500 range to reach the first-time buyer. In this market, price cuts appear to be the only way to compete. In fact, "free PCs" are available to consumers who are willing to be exposed to a significant amount of advertising.

Clearly there are times when you must engage in a preemptive strike and start a price war—or respond to a competitor's discount with a matching or deeper price cut of your own. For instance, when a competitor threatens your core business, a retaliatory price cut can be used to signify your intention to fight long and hard.

If simple retaliatory price cuts are the chosen means of defense in a price war, implement them quickly and unambiguously so competitors will know that their sales gains will be short-lived.

Similarly, when you can identify a large and growing segment of price-sensitive customers, when you have a cost advantage, when your pockets are deeper than competitors' pockets, when you can achieve economies of scale by expanding the market, or when a rival can be neutralized or eliminated because of high barriers to market entry and reentry, then engaging in price competition may be smart.

But there are several long-run implications of competing on price. First, a pattern of price cutting may teach customers to anticipate lower prices; more patient customers will defer their purchases until the next price cut. Second, a price-cutting company develops a reputation for being low-priced, and this reputation may cast doubt on the quality and image of other products under the umbrella brand and on the quality of future products. Third, price cuts have implications for other players in the market, whose self-interest may be harmed by lower prices.

If simple retaliatory price cuts are the chosen means of defense in a price war, then implement them quickly and unambiguously so competitors know that their sales gains from a price cut will be short-lived and monetarily unattractive. A slow response may prompt competitors to make additional price cuts in the future.

Retreat

On rare occasions, discretion is the better part of valor. Consequently, some businesses choose not to fight price wars; instead, they'll cede some market share rather than prolong a costly battle. 3M and DuPont are both companies that focus on developing innovations as part of their core strategy—and both have proved willing to cede share rather than participate in an unprofitable price war. In fact, 3M takes pride in the fact that roughly 40% of its revenue five years from now will come from new products. And in cases where it has retreated from pricing battles rather than standing its ground, the company seems to have come out ahead. For instance, because of withering price competition from high-volume, low-margin suppliers, 3M withdrew from the videotape business in the mid-1990s—even though videotape was invented at 3M. Similarly, Intel stopped manufacturing DRAM chips in the face of intense price competition from Taiwanese manufacturers in the 1980s, and its focus on processor chips has served it well. And Charles Schwab's decision to avoid a price war with low-priced Internet brokers has served stockholders well—the value of their Schwab holdings has more than quadrupled in the past two years.

It's Never Too Early to Prepare

It's in companies' best interests to reduce price competition because price wars can harm an entire industry. But diplomatic resolutions of price wars are generally impossible because overt diplomacy is a form of price collusion and may attract regulatory oversight. As a result, price leaders often engage in subtle forms of diplomacy that use market forces to discipline renegade companies that threaten industry profits.

Preventing a price war would be easy if it were possible to demonstrate the benefits of peace. Sadly, battle-scarred veterans who are suspicious of one another probably won't unilaterally disarm. So "price leadership" is one way to reduce industrywide price competition. Price leaders tend to develop reputations for eschewing price cuts as a way to gain market share and for responding quickly and decisively to price cutting by renegade companies. The price leaders are viewed as credible enforcers of price regimes based on their cost structures, strategic postures, or the personal characteristics of their officers. We do caution, however, that a pattern of disciplinary moves may attract unwelcome regulatory scrutiny; companies should carefully consider whether their attempts at exercising leadership may be interpreted as anticompetitive.

Price wars are a fact of life—whether we're talking about the fast-paced world of "knowledge products," the marketing of Internet appliances, or the staid, traditional business of aluminum castings. If you are not in battle currently, you probably will be fairly soon, so it's never too early to prepare.

If you are currently in a price war, understand that you can use several nonprice options to defend yourself and recognize that it is sometimes best to cede the turf under contention and seek greener pastures. If the current combatants can't be vanquished, it may be wise to observe the price war from the sidelines and enter the fray after everyone else has been eviscerated. Sometimes, to the bystanders go the spoils of war.

Price Sensitivity on the Web

INTERNET COMPANIES SUCH AS Buy.com are attempting to build market share by charging low prices. They operate under the premise that Internet shoppers are extremely sensitive to price. But the evidence to back up that assumption is mixed. On the one hand, the Web offers an easy way to search and compare prices. On the other hand, on-line shoppers tend to search for quality attributes, as well. Professors John G. Lynch of Duke University's Fuqua School of Business and Dan Ariely of MIT's Sloan School of Management have recently demonstrated that making quality information more accessible on the Web reduces price sensitivity.[2] That is why Amazon.com can charge higher prices than other on-line sites. The variety of titles it offers, the extensive product information it provides, and its reputation for rapid and reliable shipping make Amazon an easy choice for consumers who want convenience and low prices.

The growth of Internet shopping is posing interesting pricing dilemmas for bricks-and-mortar retailers. On-line vendors don't have to maintain a physical presence close to their customers, so they can operate out of a few large warehouses, thus lowering their costs. It would generally be unwise for bricks-and-mortar retailers to try to compete on price given the relatively high cost of maintaining a storefront. Instead, their strategy should emphasize features that can't be provided over the Web, such as personalized face-to-face service, browsing, immediate delivery, low-hassle returns and exchanges that don't require repackaging and shipping, and the ability to touch the product. Several retailers, such as Barnes & Noble and Tower Records, have developed an Internet presence to complement their storefronts. Such "clicks and mortar" retailers give customers the option to purchase or order on-line and then pick up the product at a bricks-and-mortar branch, and those retailers often provide a search engine in the store that is similar to their Internet offerings.

Finally, a keen understanding of consumer behavior lets some companies charge higher prices on the Web because of the anonymity that on-line transactions offer. In a recent study of 46 e-tailers of prescription drugs, the two most popular items (Viagra, a medication for erectile dysfunction, and Propecia, a medication to treat male pattern baldness) were priced roughly 10% higher than in drug stores. For obvious reasons, people prefer to have those prescriptions filled without personal contact and are willing to pay a premium for a faceless transaction.

Analyzing the Battleground

IT'S NECESSARY TO UNDERSTAND why a price war is occurring—or may occur. But it's also critical to recognize where to look for resources in battle. It's important to carefully analyze your customers, company, competitors, and other players within and outside the industry that may have an interest in how the price war plays out.

Customers and Price Sensitivity

A thoughtful evaluation of customers and their price sensitivities can provide valuable insights about whether one should fight a competitor's price cut with a price cut in kind or with some other strategy. Consumers are frequently unaware of substitute products and their prices, or they may find it difficult to make comparisons among functionally equivalent alternatives. For instance, prior to AT&T's 7-cents-a-minute plan, consumers faced a bewildering set of pricing options for long-distance phone service. AT&T charged 15 cents per minute per call with no monthly fee; or 10 cents per minute with a $4.95 monthly fee. MCI offered nighttime rates of 5 cents a minute, daytime rates of up to 25 cents a minute, and a monthly fee of $1.95. Sprint charged 5 cents per minute for nighttime calls, rates of up to 10 cents per minute for other calls, and a $5.95 monthly fee. The cost of determining the best plan when customers are unsure about their calling patterns is simply too high for a low-involvement decision like long-distance phone service. A company that wanted to compete on price could choose to simplify. That's exactly what Sprint did. It simplified its price schedule to 10 cents a minute so customers could compare its rates to those from MCI and AT&T.

Some consumers are more sensitive to quality than price, for a variety of reasons. Industrial buyers are often willing to pay more for on-time delivery or consistent quality because they need those features to make their businesses run smoother and more profitably. The very rational belief that poor quality can endanger one's health is an important reason that branded drugs command the prices they do relative to generic drugs. And snob appeal allows Davidoff to sell matches at $3.25 for a box of 40 sticks to cigar connoisseurs. The basic lesson is that different customer segments exhibit different levels of price sensitivity for different products at different times. Businesses that adopt a one-size-fits-all approach to pricing do so at their peril.

Company Abilities

Company factors such as cost structures, capabilities, and strategic positioning should also be examined carefully. Cost structures may be affected by changes in technology or business practices, which in turn may tempt a company to cut prices in a manner that will trigger a price war. For example, consider the implications of outsourcing. It's probably true that it is cheaper to buy rather than make something in-house, because the invisible hand of the marketplace will lower the acquisition price of a product. But the cost of manufacturing something in-house is largely sunk and fixed. When that product is purchased on the market, its acquisition cost is a variable one. In other words, integration can lead to a cost structure with a higher fixed-cost component and a lower variable-cost component. Consequently, the company with the lower variable costs may be tempted to reduce prices and start a price war. But even though the lower variable costs give the company an advantage, it should carefully consider whether a price war is consistent with its strategic posture. The company's lower variable costs should be used to start a price war only when it will result in the neutralization or the exit of an undesirable rival.

Consider, too, the coherence of your pricing strategy and your ability to execute it. The actions of one participant engaged in a fierce price war in the utility industry is telling: The company's senior management group asked its top manager to increase market share by 20%, return prices to profitable levels, and stabilize them. Confronted with apparently conflicting goals, the manager chose the easiest goal—build market share—which he achieved by lowering prices, thus exacerbating the price war. The directive to the manager was confusing, his resulting actions baffled competitors, and that led to considerable uncertainty and increased price turbulence in the market. When the soft costs (managerial time and attention) of changing prices through a complex supply chain were factored in, the cost of the increased market share was very dear.

The essential insight that should emerge from this exercise is whether a simple price cut is the best option given one's cost structure, capacity levels, and organizational competence.

Competitors' Response

An analysis of competitors—their cost structures, capabilities, and strategic positioning—is equally valuable. Industrywide price reductions may be appropriate under certain circumstances. But many unprofitable price wars happen because a company sees an opportunity to increase market share or profits through lower prices, while ignoring the fact that competitors will respond. Market research may reveal that sales increases following a price cut justify the action, but this same research often simply ignores competitors' price responses.

Businesses need to pay attention at the strategic level to the twin questions of who will respond and how. Smart product managers recognize the need to understand the competition and empathize with them. They project how competitors will set prices by carefully tracking historical patterns, understanding which events have triggered price changes in the past, and by tracking the timing and magnitude of price responses. They monitor public statements made by senior executives and published in company reports. And they keep their eyes peeled for activity in resource markets: competitors that acquire a new technology, labor force, information system, or distribution channel, or that form a new brand alliance, will probably make some kind of a price move that will affect other players in the industry. This sophisticated environmental scanning identifies possible adversaries and their likely modus operandi.

But which competitors should you watch? Identifying competitors often has important pricing implications. For instance, Encyclopedia Britannica discovered that its chief rival is not Grolier's Encyclopedia but Microsoft. Britannica seemed oblivious to this important competitor for several years until a steady erosion in encyclopedia sales alerted the company to startling developments in technology that changed the way consumers get information. Its books once costs thousands of dollars; Britannica now offers free access to its database on the Web and derives its revenues from banner ads, not consumers.

A company's direct competitors that share the same technology and speak to the same markets are important rivals. But indirect competitors that satisfy customer needs through the use of different technologies and that have completely different cost structures are perhaps the most dangerous. In fact, direct competitors such as major airlines frequently coexist quite peacefully. Examining their pricing-decision rules suggests why. U.S. Department of Transportation studies indicate that when one hub-based airline enters another's hub, it typically does not engage in price-based competition because it fears retaliation in its own hub. Conversely, price wars may often be started by a company from an entirely different industry, with a radically different technology, whose cost advantages give it enough leverage to enter your market and steal your share.

The process of identifying competitors also reveals the strengths and weaknesses of current and potential rivals. This has important implications for how a company competes. It is generally wise to not stir a hornet's nest by starting a price war with a competitor that has a significantly larger resource base or a reputation for being a fierce price warrior. When analyzing your competition, carefully determine who they are, how price fits with their strategic position, how they make pricing decisions, and what their capabilities and resources are.

Contributors, Collaborators, and Other Interested Parties

Finally, it is important to monitor other players in the industry whose self-interest or profiles may affect outcomes. Suppliers, distributors, providers of complementary goods and services, customers, government agencies, and so on contribute significantly to the consumption experience, including product quality, the sales pitch, and after-sales service. They often wield considerable influence on the outcome of a price war—directly or indirectly. Sometimes these contributors may provide the impetus for, or may indirectly start, a price war. Motorola discovered as much when it introduced low-priced cellular phones in China and Brazil. Soon Motorola observed that the street price for its phones had dropped substantially in the United States. Distributors were diverting products bound for China and Brazil to the profitable U.S. and European markets; sometimes the products never even left the dock. Motorola's distributors had created a "gray market" because Motorola had given them a reason to believe that prices in the United States were too high.

Sometimes contributors can help reduce price competition by enhancing the product's value, as Intel does for computer manufacturers; assisting with marketing, as airline frequent-flyer programs do for credit-card companies; and limiting the exposure to competing products, as MITI has done for Japanese companies facing international competition at home. Smart managers must carefully consider other players and their interests (profit margins for suppliers and distributors, commissions for sales representatives, and so on) before starting a price war or joining one.

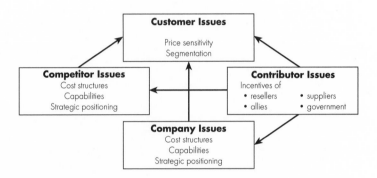

Notes

1. See Carl Shapiro and Hal Varian, "Versioning: The Smart Way to Sell Information," HBR November–December 1998.

2. See "Wine Online: Search Costs and Competition on Price, Quality, and Distribution," *Marketing Science*, 2000.

Originally published in March–April 2000
Reprint R00208

Contextual Marketing

The Real Business of the Internet

DAVID KENNY AND JOHN F. MARSHALL

Executive Summary

THE PAINFUL TRUTH is that the Internet has been a let-down for most companies—largely because the dominant model for Internet commerce, the destination Web site, doesn't suit the needs for those companies or their customers. Most consumer product companies don't provide enough value or dynamic information to induce customers to make the repeat visits—and disclose the detailed information—that make such sites profitable.

In this article, David Kenny and John F. Marshall suggest the companies discard the notion that a Web site equals an Internet strategy. Instead of trying to create destinations that people will come to, companies need to use the power and reach of the Internet to deliver tailored messages and information to customers. Companies have to become what the authors call "contextual marketers."

Delivering the most relevant information possible to consumers in the most timely manner possible will become feasible, the authors say, as access moves beyond the PC to shopping malls, retail stores, airports, bus stations, and even cars. The authors describe how the ubiquitous Internet will hasten the demise of the destination Web site—and open up scads of opportunities to reach customers through marketing "mobilemediaries," such as smart cards, e-wallets, and bar code scanners.

The companies that master the complexity of the ubiquitous Internet will gain significant advantages: they'll gain greater intimacy with customers and target market segments more efficiently. The ones that don't will be dismissed as nuisances, the authors conclude. They suggest ways to become welcome additions—not unwelcome intrusions—to customers' lives.

T IME FOR A PAINFUL ADMISSION: the Internet has been a letdown for most companies. Certainly, the Web is at the top of corporate America's priority list—the $10 billion that large U.S. companies spent on Web site development in 1999 is evidence enough of that. Yet in any given month, only about half of the largest U.S. consumer businesses attract more than 400,000 site visitors—and a similar percentage of sites generate no commercial revenue at all.

If the economic return is minimal, the strategic payoff is even lower. Less than half of these corporate sites capture any self-reported customer data. The few sites that manage to gather any information do a pretty poor job of it—we estimate that they compile meaningful profiles on less than 1% of their customers. And despite all assurances to the contrary, the Web is rarely a low-cost customer acquisition channel. Most companies using standard "drive-to-site" Web marketing approaches, such as banner advertisements, quickly learn that their customer acquisition costs are greater than those in the physical world—often 1.5 to 2.5 times greater.

Most corporate Web sites fall short of managers' high expectations because of a fundamental mismatch—the dominant model for Internet commerce, the destination Web site, simply doesn't suit the needs of most companies or their customers. For a destination Web site to make economic sense, it must attract repeat visits from customers, with each visit adding ever greater increments of information to a customer's profile. For example, Amazon.com's business model is based on retaining each customer for a significant number of years—up to an astonishing 12 years by some analysts' forecasts. That is considered sufficient time to develop the deep, continuing relationships that will justify the company's heavy investment in its site. Such a model is well suited to providers of financial services and travel services, whose dynamic, information-driven offerings generate repeat site visits that yield an increasingly detailed customer profile. But at the other extreme, most consumer product companies face an insurmountable challenge in adopting the destination site model; they don't provide enough value to induce consumers to make repeat visits, much less disclose intimate information.

Does this mean the Internet is of no value to all but a handful of well-positioned companies? Not at all. What it does mean is that most companies need to discard the notion that a Web site equals an Internet strategy. Instead of trying to create destinations that people will come to, they need to use the power and reach of the

Internet to deliver tailored messages and information to customers at the point of need. They need to become what we call *contextual marketers.*

The Ubiquitous Internet

Hastening the demise of the destination site model is the phenomenon we call the *ubiquitous Internet.* Within three to five years, the Internet will begin to be accessible from almost anywhere. Consumers will be linked to the Net via wireless telephones, personal digital assistants, interactive television, always-on DSL or cable, or laptop computers with wireless connections. Consumers will be constantly enveloped in a digital environment—a personal digital bubble, as it were. And the phenomenon extends well beyond personal devices. Car makers, shopping mall operators, plane manufacturers, retailers, airport officials, and bus station managers all have plans on the drawing board—or under way—to provide Internet access to their customers. A quick look outside the United States confirms that this ubiquity is approaching at warp speed: already in Japan, the largest Internet service provider is a wireless carrier.

As the Internet becomes ubiquitous, companies will gain many new ways to connect with customers. This explosion of access will open up enormous marketing opportunities, but it will also pose big challenges. Designing a compelling Web site may be hard, and using personalization software to customize what individual consumers see may be tougher still. But these tasks pale in comparison to managing a pervasive electronic presence that senses and responds not only to who the customer is but where she is and what she's doing. (See "Before and After: What Lies Ahead for Web Marketing.")

Before and After

What Lies Ahead for Web Marketing

In three to five years, the ubiquitous Internet will begin to unfold. Consumers will be constantly enveloped in a digital environment, and marketing strategies will have to change radically. Web sites, the centerpiece of most of today's strategies, will be only one piece of a much larger and more complex puzzle.

	Today's Internet	Ubiquitous Internet
Intermediary	• The destination Web site	• The mobilemediary
Access Points	• PC equipped with Web browser	• PDA • e-wallet • wireless phone • kiosks • interactive TV • Internet-enabled POS terminal • always-on broadband
Customers Can Be Reached	• Only when they're sitting at their PCs browsing the Web	• 24 hours a day, seven days a week, anywhere on the planet—in their cars, at the mall, on an airplane, at a sports arena
Customer Focus	• Price-conscious comparison shoppers	• Anyone with an immediate need, who will spend money to save time
Strategic Mandate	• Focus on content • Build destination Web site • Personalize Web pages • Wait (and wait) for customers to show up	• Focus on context • Build ubiquitous agent that travels alongside your customer • Master technology that lets you know when you're needed • Be there when and where your customer is ready to buy

Think about airlines—they need Web sites so their
customers can make reservations and check schedules
on-line. But the airlines will also need much more. When
a traveler needs to change plans midjourney, an airline
must be able to provide for him an Internet-enabled
mobile device while he's still in the air or a computer terminal while he's in the departure lounge or airline club.
The passenger may also require related services—hotel
reservations and ground transportation, for instance—
that change as his plans change.

For their part, retailers may use kiosks, Internet-
enabled point-of-sale (POS) terminals, or mobile devices
to digitally recognize loyal customers while they're
in a store. Then, before the customer has even reached
the checkout counter, the retailer can devise special
offers based on the customer's purchase history and
preferences.

The companies that master the complexity of the
ubiquitous Internet will gain significant advantages:
greater intimacy with customers and more efficient targeting of market segments. And by offering customers a
more valuable, more timely product, they'll be able to
charge a premium price. The crucial step is to recognize
that the ubiquitous Internet will further reconfigure
value chains that have already been shattered by the
Internet's first wave. As the ubiquitous Internet becomes
a reality, a new kind of intermediary role emerges—we
call it the *mobilemediary*.

The mobilemediary will be able to break into the
value chain at any point, bringing information and transaction capabilities to customers whenever and wherever
they're ready to buy a product or avail themselves of a
service. Mobilemediaries might serve up your spouse's

wish list when you're in the mall shopping for a birthday present. They might enable you to trade stocks when the market is plunging and your commuter train is stalled. When you're with your family at a theme park, they might let you know that it's your turn to ride the roller coaster. But whatever form these intermediaries take, they'll be less about content and more about context.

The Rise of Contextual Marketing

Contextual marketing opens up opportunities for companies that, for various reasons, can't form the ongoing digital relationships that are the lifeblood of a successful destination Web site—for example, makers of consumer packaged goods, single-product companies, and infrequent service providers.

The most innovative of these companies are already adapting their marketing strategies to take advantage of the ubiquitous Internet. Take Mobil's Speedpass: the digital wand can be attached to a keychain and lets customers pay for gas and other purchases by waving it in front of an electronic reader at the gas pump or at the checkout counter. It has proved so convenient that some drivers go miles out of their way to find a filling station that accepts Speedpass. In Japan, wireless carrier NTT DoCoMo has signed up a staggering 10 million consumers for its i-mode service over the past 12 months. I-mode offers subscribers wireless access to restaurant locators, ski-condition reports, hotel reservations systems, on-line auctions, and thousands of other services. Some of this information is already available on the World Wide Web, but with i-mode, consumers can tee up the information they want when they want it, not just when they're sitting at their PCs. Japanese consumer marketers are taking advantage of this situation—there are now almost 10,000 i-mode sites.

As these examples suggest, the ubiquitous Internet will vastly expand marketers' opportunities to reach customers. At the same time, it will destabilize the "four Ps" of traditional marketing: price, product, placement, and promotion will all be thrown into constant flux, depending on the customer and the context. The marketing goal will be the same as ever: deliver the right product to the right customer at the right time. Companies will still have to form a deep understanding of their customers' needs and desires. But in many cases, instead of owning customer data or individual customer relationships, successful contextual marketers will borrow them.

Recent initiatives by Johnson & Johnson demonstrate this kind of contextual marketing in action. Accepting that it was unlikely to develop a meaningful dialogue with most consumers about headache remedies, skin care products, and the like, the health-care-product manufacturer has chosen not to focus its strategies and investments on a Web site alone. Instead, it places its products in the most fruitful digital context possible. Banner ads for J&J's Tylenol headache reliever unfurl on e-brokers' sites whenever the stock market falls by more than 100 points. The brokerage firms own the customer relationships, but J&J breaks into the dialogue at the moment when its marketing opportunity is greatest.

Or consider J&J's campaign for Clean & Clear, a skin care product line for teenage girls. Resisting the temptation to create yet another ill-fated destination site, such as the definitive on-line source for all things acne-related, J&J establishes a presence within preexisting on-line teen communities. The company gives teenage girls, many of whom spend their free time chatting on-line, the chance to send one another talking electronic postcards that offer a free skin analysis and a sample of Clean & Clear. The campaign's viral component—friend-to-friend referrals that multiply exponentially—significantly increases the product's exposure at little additional cost. The result: a response rate that's several times higher than standard Web levels, without any significant site investments. Once again, J&J inserts itself into a preexisting relationship at the optimal moment.

Even companies with flourishing destination sites can benefit from contextual marketing. Dell Computer, whose own site is an e-commerce leader, recognizes that most on-line computer shoppers bypass Dell's site and go straight to ZDNet and CNET for in-depth product information—combined, those two sites have almost ten times the number of site visitors that Dell has. So instead of using costly and ineffective banner ads to divert sales prospects to its own site, Dell posts its detailed product information on ZDNet's and CNET's sites. Visitors at those sites can then compare the latest offerings from Dell and Compaq, pick the Dell machine, and launch the ordering process directly from the CNET or ZDNet site. By piggybacking on CNET's and ZDNet's relationships, Dell has significantly improved its customer acquisition economics.

Beyond the Web Site

For all their innovation and ingenuity, J&J's and Dell's contextual marketing efforts are still defined by, and confined to, the PC. But the "tethered" Web is just a limited slice of the Internet, and it is ill suited to the marketing needs of many companies. The latest Internet technologies expose points of contact that are infinitely more timely and relevant. The convergence of the Internet with broadband connectivity and with TV will let marketers integrate commerce and entertainment: if you like Regis's suit, order it with a couple of clicks of your remote. Don't laugh—although early experiments with interactive TV were an expensive bust, recent trials have been more encouraging. When an interactive TV performance by pop artist Melissa Etheridge included an on-screen promotion for her latest CD, it generated an astonishing 46% click-through rate. The average click-through rate for a Web-based banner ad is only 0.5% at best.

Opportunities for contextual marketing extend well beyond the home. Mobile devices and Internet access in a broad range of public venues will let contextual marketers link real-life situations to virtual information and offerings. For instance, Unilever's mobile recipe book concept, which will be available on digital phones in Europe, should influence consumers' packaged-goods decisions far more than the company's Web site ever could. Intended for use while shopping, the mobile tool suggests recipes and breaks them down into their ingredients—identified, wherever possible, by their Unilever brand name. Rather than try to establish an ongoing Web site relationship with European grocery shoppers, U.K.-based Unilever plans to give them a digital tool precisely when and where they need it, helping shoppers and promoting Unilever brands at the same time.

Companies that practice contextual marketing should be guided by the following imperative: don't try to bring the customer to a Web site, bring the message directly to the customer at the point of need.

Conceivably, the mobile recipe book could be used in connection with mobile e-coupons—electronic sales promotions that take into account the customer's identity and location, among other variables, and that are issued as close to the point of sale as possible. These time-sensitive contextual promotions can influence consumer purchasing decisions. At the same time, they let companies vary their pricing in real time in response to market and supply conditions.

These are just some of the ways that consumer product companies can harness the power of the ubiquitous Internet. But however they reach customers, whatever the mobilemediary, these companies should be guided by the following imperative: don't try to bring the customer to the site; instead, bring the message directly to the customer at the point of need.

The Ubiquitous Relationship

Even companies with enduring customer relationships and heavily trafficked Web sites need to master the tools of contextual marketing: electronic wallets, smart cards, mobile shopping lists, Internet-enabled POS systems, and many other electronic utilities and access technologies. These tools can extend the reach of relationship-oriented companies beyond their Web sites, capturing more information and improving customer service in the virtual and the physical worlds.

Consider FedEx. The company never fell into the trap of designating its Web site as its only mechanism for managing digital customer relationships—not surprising given that FedEx was practicing contextual marketing before the Web even existed. As early as 1988, its proprietary PowerShip terminals, installed in customers' mail rooms, brought digital interactions to the point of need.

Today, FedEx is creating even deeper relationships. Its customers can use mobile devices to track packages or to locate the nearest spots to drop them off. Soon it will be possible for customers anywhere in the world to use a mobile phone to create a shipping label or a digital tracking record for a package.

The FedEx mobilemediaries could alert the company's customers to shipping problems encountered in transit. For instance, if a time-sensitive package is being held up at customs for lack of documentation, the mobilemediary could inform the customer and route the appropriate electronic forms to the customs office. FedEx also envisions customers using chip-embedded smart cards that can generate shipping labels and tracking information when swiped through a service terminal. Eventually, ubiquitous intelligence could move into the packages themselves; "smart packages" embedded with location-sensitive chips could transmit real-time tracking information to shippers and recipients, further expanding loyalty and raising competitors' barriers to entry.

American Express, for its part, recognizes that there's far more to the digital relationship than the customer's occasional visit to the company's site to review a bill. Ideally, the relationship should deepen every time the customer uses his or her Amex card. That's why the company has developed an e-wallet that automates the process of entering a customer's on-line purchasing data, such as her credit card number and shipping information. The e-wallet fosters loyalty by relieving the customer of that tedious chore. Even more important, it could become a tool for capturing data and cross selling at the point of purchase. With explicit consent from customers, their e-wallet could follow them as they surf the

Web or access the Internet through their mobile devices. The result would be a trove of customer intelligence.

Amex's recently launched Blue card is a potential predecessor to the ubiquitous e-wallet. With its embedded smart chip, the Blue card could extend beyond the Web site to the physical point of sale, bringing customer profile data not just to American Express, but also to the more than six million merchants that accept the company's cards.

But digital relationship management will involve far more than simply multiplying the points of contact. Ubiquity will enable bricks-and-mortar companies to convert physical customer traffic into digital relationships, introducing new combatants to the already fierce war for eyeballs. These companies will be able to use their physical access to customers to deliver precisely targeted messages—their own as well as those of companies that borrow the point of contact. Airlines, for instance, have a captive audience in the terminal club, the departure lounge, and the plane itself. They can exploit this advantage to offer contextual services beyond the reach of virtual agents such as Travelocity or Trip.com.

Even quintessential bricks-and-mortar businesses such as parking garages and shopping malls will be able to turn their traffic into personal relationships and incremental revenue. The best-conceived Web sites in the world wouldn't significantly improve the fortunes of those businesses. But ubiquity now allows garages and malls to manage customer relationships directly. In Sweden, garages now accept payment from the "digital wallet" of a Sonera cell phone. Embedded in the digital money is significant information about garage customers, including their names and when and how often they park. Garage owners can use the data to turn frequent visitors into monthly customers and to engage in dynamic pricing, charging more when the garage is nearly full and less when business is slow.

For shopping mall operators, ubiquity creates an opportunity to manage the customer relationships previously owned by individual retail tenants. Simon Properties, the largest retail mall developer in the United States, gives some shoppers mobile devices that they can use to generate electronic wish lists or to order products for home delivery. Simon eventually will be able to track shoppers as they move through the mall, feeding tenant retailers the purchase data they need to offer timely and relevant promotions. No longer an anonymous provider of retail space, Simon can now add value to the retail experience by helping store owners better match their products and services with customers' needs.

Ubiquity creates opportunities wherever there is customer traffic. As an extension of its existing FastPass electronic ticketing system, Disney could win loyalty in its theme parks by creating virtual lines. Using a Disney-supplied mobile device, a customer could reserve a seat on a popular ride hours in advance, eliminating the time spent waiting in line. That would increase customer enjoyment (and spending) while deepening the information-based relationship. Drawing on the information gathered during the customer's visit to the park, Disney could follow up with carefully targeted catalogs or promotions for movies, games, or merchandise. In similar fashion, some pretty unlikely candidates—from sports stadiums to movie theaters to taxicabs—suddenly emerge as digital intermediaries.

The automobile may present the richest new opportunity for digital relationship management. The ubiquitous

Internet could enable GM, the world's largest manufacturing company, to transform itself from an automaker
to a communications intermediary. After all, drivers
spend an average of 8.5 hours a week inside the approxi-
mately 70 million GM vehicles on the road today. By
comparison, America Online's 22 million subscribers
spend 7.5 hours a week on-line. The information in every
one of GM's vehicles is immensely valuable to other marketers. Shell and Texaco, for instance, would pay good
money to know how much gas is left in a car's tank.
Retailers and restaurateurs would pay to know when a
vehicle is passing nearby. Mechanics would pay for
access to a GM vehicle's service history. By reconceiving
the car as an information device, GM dramatically
increases the amount of value it can capture from each
vehicle, while providing services that tie car owners
closer to the company.

The New Corporate Agenda

It's tempting to take a wait-and-see attitude to the
ubiquitous Internet. Wireless technologies are still in
development. Interactive
TV is years away from
mass adoption. E-coupons
and other methods of
reaching the customer at
the point of sale are in
their infancy. But now is
the time to begin building
the skills needed to win in the age of ubiquity.

*Ubiquity will allow
businesses to accompany
their customers 24
hours a day, but not every
business will be invited
along for the ride.*

   Senior managers need to start by honestly assessing
their business. Does it offer a service or a product that
will generate repeat visits to a Web site? Does it stand a

chance of forming an ongoing relationship with customers? If so, the company should spend what it takes to design and build a destination Web site. But for most companies, the customer relationship is a series of contextual interactions. Those companies shouldn't be afraid to define an Internet strategy that de-emphasizes the site itself; there are better ways for them to spend their marketing dollars.

Ubiquity will allow businesses to accompany their customers 24 hours a day, but not every business will be invited along for the ride. Customers will admit only the most relevant messages into their lives, so the concept of adding value to customers' lives will change significantly in an always-on world. The companies that can anticipate and meet the real needs of their customers—based on where they are located, what they do, and which communities of interest they belong to—will be valued partners. The companies that can't will be dismissed as pesky nuisances.

The winning companies will be the ones that master a few critical disciplines. First, database marketing tools will be essential. Whatever their industry, mass marketers will have to become direct marketers because the ubiquitous Internet will require companies to constantly retarget and retailor their messages. Second, new technology skills need to be mastered quickly: the companies that build new databases, upgrade their legacy systems early, and create the middleware necessary to tailor their messages to customers' ever-changing needs and situations will move ahead of the competition. And finally, companies need to adopt the discipline of measurement. Winners will measure everything, constantly refining their messages to meet ever-heightening consumer demands for relevance.

Mastering the contextual possibilities of the ubiquitous Internet will require a significant commitment of corporate resources. But the payoff is just as significant: Internet strategies that are truly relevant to companies and their customers. It will be neither cheap nor easy, but it will be a far better investment than pouring $10 billion into Web sites that few people visit.

Originally published in November–December 2000
Reprint R00608

The Lure of Global Branding

DAVID A. AAKER AND
ERICH JOACHIMSTHALER

Executive Summary

AS MORE AND MORE COMPANIES begin to see the
world as their market, brand builders look with envy
upon those businesses that appear to have created
global brands—brands whose positioning, advertising
strategy, personality, look, and feel are in most respects
the same from one country to another. Attracted by such
high-profile examples of success, these companies want
to globalize their own brands.

But that's a risky path to follow, according to David
Aaker and Erich Joachimsthaler. Why? Because creating
strong global brands takes global brand leadership. It
can't be done simply by edict from on high. Specifically,
companies must use organizational structures, processes,
and cultures to allocate brand-building resources globally, to create global synergies, and to develop a global
brand strategy that coordinates and leverages country
brand strategies.

87

Aaker and Joachimsthaler offer four prescriptions for companies seeking to achieve global brand leadership. First, companies must stimulate the sharing of insights and best practices across countries—a system in which "it won't work here" attitudes can be overcome. Second, companies should support a common global brand-planning process, one that is consistent across markets and products. Third, they should assign global managerial responsibility for brands in order to create cross-country synergies and to fight local bias. And fourth, they need to execute brilliant brand-building strategies.

Before stampeding blindly toward global branding, companies need to think through the systems they have in place. Otherwise, any success they achieve is likely to be random—and that's a fail-safe recipe for mediocrity.

As MORE AND MORE COMPANIES come to view the entire world as their market, brand builders look with envy upon those that appear to have created global brands—brands whose positioning, advertising strategy, personality, look, and feel are in most respects the same from one country to another. It's easy to understand why. Even though most global brands are not absolutely identical from one country to another—Visa changes its logo in some countries; Heineken means something different in the Netherlands than it does abroad—companies whose brands have become more global reap some clear benefits.

Consider for a moment the economies of scale enjoyed by IBM. It costs IBM much less to create a single global advertising campaign than it would to create separate campaigns for dozens of markets. And because IBM uses only one agency for all its global advertising, it carries a lot of clout with the agency and can get the most talented people working on its behalf. A global brand also benefits from being driven by a single strategy. Visa's unvarying "worldwide acceptance" position, for example, is much easier for the company to manage than dozens of country-specific strategies.

Consolidating all advertising into one agency and developing a global theme can cause problems that outweigh any advantages.

Attracted by such high-profile examples of success, many companies are tempted to try to globalize their own brands. The problem is, that goal is often unrealistic. Consolidating all advertising into one agency and developing a global advertising theme—often the cornerstone of the effort—can cause problems that outweigh any advantages. And edicts from on high—"Henceforth, use only brand-building programs that can be applied across countries"—can prove ineffective or even destructive. Managers who stampede blindly toward creating a global brand without considering whether such a move fits well with their company or their markets risk falling over a cliff. There are several reasons for that.

First, economies of scale may prove elusive. It is sometimes cheaper and more effective for companies to create ads locally than to import ads and then adapt them for each market. Moreover, cultural differences may make it hard to pull off a global campaign: even the best agency may have trouble executing it well in all countries. Finally, the potential cost savings from "media spillover"—in which, for example, people in France view German television ads—have been exaggerated. Language barriers and cultural differences have made realizing such benefits difficult for most companies.

Second, forming a successful global brand team can prove difficult. Developing a superior brand strategy for one country is challenging enough; creating one that can be applied worldwide can be daunting (assuming one even exists). Teams face several stumbling blocks: they need to gather and understand a great deal of information; they must be extremely creative; and they need to anticipate a host of challenges in execution. Relatively few teams will be able to meet all those challenges.

Third, global brands can't just be imposed on all markets. For example, a brand's image may not be the same throughout the world. Honda means quality and reliability in the United States, but in Japan, where quality is a given for most cars, Honda represents speed, youth, and energy. And consider market position. In Britain, where Ford is number one, the company positioned its Galaxy minivan as the luxurious "nonvan" in order to appeal not only to soccer moms but also to executives. But in Germany, where Volkswagen rules, Ford had to position the Galaxy as "the clever alternative." Similarly, Cadbury in the United Kingdom and Milka in Germany have preempted the associations that connect milk with chocolate; thus neither company could implement a global positioning strategy.

For all those reasons, taking a more nuanced approach is the better course of action. Developing global brands should not be the priority. Instead, companies should work on creating strong brands in all markets through global brand leadership.

Global brand leadership means using organizational structures, processes, and cultures to allocate brand-building resources globally, to create global synergies, and to develop a global brand strategy that coordinates and leverages country brand strategies. That is, of course, easier said than done. For example, companies tend to give the bulk of their brand-building attention to countries with large sales—at the expense of emerging markets that may represent big opportunities. But some companies have successfully engaged in global brand management. To find out how, we interviewed executives from 35 companies in the United States, Europe, and Japan that have successfully developed strong brands across countries. (About half the executives were from companies that made frequently purchased consumer products; the rest represented durables, high-tech products, and service brands.)

Four common ideas about effective brand leadership emerged from those interviews. Companies must:

- stimulate the sharing of insights and best practices across countries;

- support a common global brand-planning process;

- assign managerial responsibility for brands in order to create cross-country synergies and to fight local bias; and

- execute brilliant brand-building strategies.

Sharing Insights and Best Practices

A companywide communication system is the most basic element of global brand leadership. Managers from country to country need to be able to find out about programs that have worked or failed elsewhere; they also need a way to easily give and receive knowledge about customers—knowledge that will vary from one market to another.

Creating such a system is harder than it sounds. Busy people usually have little motivation to take the time to explain why efforts have been successful or ineffective; furthermore, they'd rather not give out information that may leave them exposed to criticism. Another problem is one that everyone in business faces today: information overload. And a feeling of "it won't work here" often pervades companies that attempt to encourage the sharing of market knowledge.

To overcome those problems, companies must nurture and support a culture in which best practices are freely communicated. In addition, people and procedures must come together to create a rich base of knowledge that is relevant and easy to access. Offering incentives is one way to get people to share what they know. American Management Systems, for example, keeps track of the employees who post insights and best practices and rewards them during annual performance reviews.

Regular meetings can be an effective way of communicating insights and best practices. Frito-Lay, for example, sponsors a "market university" roughly three times a year in which 35 or so marketing directors and general managers from around the world meet in Dallas for a week. The university gets people to think about brand leadership concepts, helps people overcome the mind-set of "I am different—global programs won't work in my market," and creates a group of people around the world who believe in and understand brands and brand strategy. During the week, country managers present case studies on packaging, advertising, and promotions that were tested in one country and then successfully applied in another. The case studies demonstrate that practices can be transferred even when a local marketing team is skeptical.

Formal meetings are useful, but true learning takes place during informal conversations and gatherings. And the personal relationships that people establish during those events are often more important than the information they share. Personal ties lead to meaningful exchanges down the road that can foster brand-building programs.

In addition to staging meetings, companies are increasingly using intranets to communicate insights and best practices. (Sharing such information by e-mail isn't as effective—there is simply too much e-mail clutter. E-mail is useful, however, for conveying breaking news about competitors or new technology.) The key is to have a team create a knowledge bank on an intranet that is valuable and accessible to those who need it. Mobil, for example, uses a set of best-practice networks to do just that. The networks connect people in the company (and sometimes from partner organizations) who are experts on, for example, new product introduction, brand architecture, and retail-site presentation. Each network has a senior management sponsor and a leader who actively solicits postings from the experts. The leader ensures that the information is formatted, organized, and posted on an easy-to-use intranet site.

Field visits are another useful way to learn about best practices. Honda sends teams to "live with best practices" and to learn how they work. In some companies, the CEO travels to different markets in order to energize the country teams and to see best practices in action.

Procter & Gamble uses worldwide strategic-planning groups of three to 20 people for each category to encourage and support global strategies. The teams have several tasks. They mine local knowledge about markets and disseminate that information globally. They gather data about effective country-specific marketing efforts and encourage testing elsewhere. They create global manufacturing sourcing strategies. And they develop policies that dictate which aspects of the brand strategy must be followed everywhere and which ones are up to country management.

Another way that companies can communicate information about their brands is by sharing research. Ford operates very differently from country to country in Europe, but its businesses share research methods and findings. Ford UK, for example, which is very skilled at doing direct mail and research on segmentation, makes its technology and research methods available to other countries. That's especially important for businesses in small markets that are short on budget and staff.

Supporting Global Brand Planning

Two years ago, the newly appointed global brand manager of a prominent packaged-goods marketer organized a brand strategy review. He found that all the country brand managers used their own vocabularies and strategy templates and had their own strategies. The resulting mess had undoubtedly contributed to inferior marketing and weakened brands. Another packaged-goods company tried to avoid that problem by developing a global planning system. Brand managers weren't given incentives or trained properly to use the system, however, and the result was inconsistent, half-hearted efforts at planning.

Companies that practice global brand management use a planning process that is consistent across markets and products—a brand presentation looks and sounds the same whether it's delivered in Singapore, Spain, or Sweden, and whether it's for PCs or printers. It shares the same well-defined vocabulary, strategic analysis inputs (such as competitor positions and strategies), brand strategy model, and outputs (such as brand-building programs).

There is no one accepted process model, but all models have two starting points: it must be clear which person or group is responsible for the brand and the brand strategy, and a process template must exist. The completed template should specify such aspects of a strategy as the target segment, the brand identity or vision, brand equity goals and measures, and brand-building programs that will be used within and outside the company. Although various process models can work, observations of effective programs suggest five guidelines.

First, the process should include an analysis of customers, competitors, and the brand. Analysis of customers must go beyond quantitative market research data; managers need to understand the brand associations that resonate with people. Analysis of competitors is necessary to differentiate the brand and to ensure that its communication program—which may include sponsorship, promotion, and advertising—doesn't simply copy what other companies are doing. And an audit of the brand itself involves an examination of its heritage, image, strengths, and problems, as well as the company's vision for it. The brand needs to reflect that vision to avoid making empty promises.

Second, the process should avoid a fixation on product attributes. A narrow focus on attributes leads to short-lived, easily copied advantages and to shallow customer relationships. Most strong brands go beyond functional benefits; despite what customers might say, a brand can also deliver emotional benefits and help people express themselves. A litmus test of whether a company really understands its brands is whether it incorporates the following elements into the brand strategy: brand personality (how the brand would be described if it were a person), user imagery (how the brand's typical user is perceived), intangibles that are associated with the company (its perceived innovativeness or reputation for quality, for example), and symbols associated with the brand, such as Virgin's Branson, the Coke bottle, or the Harley eagle. A simple three-word phrase or a brief list of product attributes cannot adequately represent a strong brand.

Third, the process must include programs to communicate the brand's identity (what the brand should stand for) to employees and company partners. Without clarity and enthusiasm internally about the associations the brand aspires to develop, brand building has no chance. A brand manual often plays a key role. Unilever has a detailed manual on its most global brand, Lipton Tea, that puts the answer to any question about its brand identity (What does the brand stand for? What are the timeless elements of the brand? What brand-building programs are off target?) at the fingertips of all employees. Other companies use workshops (Nestlé), newsletters (Hewlett-Packard), books (Volvo), and videos (the Limited) to communicate brand identity. To engage people in this process, Mobil asked employees to nominate recent programs or actions that best reflected the core elements of the Mobil brand—leadership, partnership, and trust. The employees with the best nominations were honored guests at a car race sponsored by the company.

Fourth, the process must include brand equity measurement and goals. Without measurement, brand building is often just talk; yet surprisingly few companies have systems that track brand equity. Pepsi is an exception. In the mid-1990s, Pepsi introduced a system based on what it calls a "marketplace P&L." The P&L measures brand equity by tracking the results of blind taste tests, the extent of a product's distribution, and the results of customer opinion surveys about the brand. In the beginning, country managers were strongly encouraged—but not required—to use the system. But the value of the marketplace P&L soon become clear, as country managers compared results at meetings and used the shared information to improve their brand-building efforts. In 1998, CEO Roger Enrico made the system mandatory—a dramatic indication of its value given Pepsi's decentralized culture and the home office's general reluctance to impose companywide rules.

Finally, the process must include a mechanism that ties global brand strategies to country brand strategies. Sony and Mobil, among others, use a top-down approach. They begin with a global brand strategy; country strategies follow from it. A country brand strategy might augment the global strategy by adding elements to modify the brand's identity. For example, if the manager of a Mobil fuel brand in Brazil wants to emphasize that the brand gives an honest gallon (because other brands of fuel in Brazil are not considered reliable in their measurements), he would add "honest measures" to the country brand identity. Or a country brand strategist might put a different spin on an element of the brand's identity. For example, although the term "leadership" may mean "technology leadership" in most countries, the strategist may change it to mean "market leadership" in his or her market. In the top-down approach, the country brand team has the burden of justifying any departures from the global brand strategy.

In the bottom-up approach, the global brand strategy is built from the country brand strategies. Country strategies are grouped by similarities. A grouping might, for example, be made on the basis of market maturity (underdeveloped, emerging, or developed) or competitive context (whether the brand is a leader or a challenger). While the brand strategy for these groupings will differ, a global brand strategy should also be able to identify common elements. Over time, the number of distinct strategies will usually fall as experiences and best practices are shared. As the number shrinks, the company can capture synergies. Mercedes, for example, uses one advertising agency to create a menu of five campaigns. Brand managers in different countries can then pick the most suitable campaign for their market.

Assigning Responsibility

Local managers often believe that their situation is unique—and therefore, that insights and best practices from other countries can't be applied to their markets. Their belief is based in part on justifiable confidence in their knowledge of the country, the competitive milieu, and the consumers. Any suggestion that such confidence is misplaced can feel threatening. Moreover, people are comfortable with strategies that have already proven effective. The local brand managers may fear that they will be coerced or enticed into following a strategy that doesn't measure up to their current efforts.

Most companies today have a decentralized culture and structure. They find it difficult, therefore, to persuade country teams to quickly and voluntarily accept and implement a global best practice. To ensure that local teams overcome such reluctance, an individual or group must be in charge of the global brand. Our research suggests that responsibility for global brand leadership can follow four possible configurations: business management team, brand champion, global brand manager, and global brand team. The first two are led by senior executives; the latter two by middle managers.

BUSINESS MANAGEMENT TEAM

This approach is most suitable when the company's top managers are marketing or branding people who regard brands as the key asset to their business. P&G fits that description. Each of its 11 product categories is run by a global category team. The teams consist of the four managers who have line responsibility for R&D, manufacturing, and marketing for the category within their region. Each team is chaired by an executive vice president who also has a second line job. For example, the head of health and beauty aids in Europe also chairs the hair care global category team. The teams meet five or six times a year.

Because the teams are made up of top-level line executives, there are no organizational barriers to carrying out decisions. At the country level, P&G's brand and advertising managers implement the strategy. Thus local bias cannot get in the way of the company's global brand leadership.

The 11 teams strive to create global brands without weakening brand strength locally. They define the identity and position of brands in their categories throughout the world. They encourage local markets to test and

adopt brand-building programs that have been successful elsewhere. And they decide which brands will get new
product advances. For example, Elastesse, the chemical
compound that helps people eliminate "helmet head,"
was first added to the company's Pantene product line
rather than one of its three sister brands.

BRAND CHAMPION

This is a senior executive, possibly the CEO, who serves
as the brand's primary advocate and nurturer. The
approach is particularly well suited to companies whose
top executives have a passion and talent for brand strategy. Companies like Sony, Gap, Beiersdorf (Nivea), and
Nestlé meet that description. Nestlé has a brand champion for each of its 12 corporate strategic brands. As is
true for the leaders of P&G's business management
teams, each brand champion at Nestlé has a second
assignment. Thus the vice president for nutrition is the
brand champion for Carnation, and the vice president
for instant coffee is the brand champion for Taster's
Choice (known as Nescafé outside the United States). At
Nestlé, brand leadership is not just talk. The additional
work that the brand champion takes on has resulted in a
change in the company's performance-evaluation and
compensation policies.

A brand champion approves all brand-stretching
decisions (to put the Carnation label on a white milk
chocolate bar, for example) and monitors the presentation of the brand worldwide. He or she must be familiar
with local contexts and managers, identify insights and
best practices, and propagate them through sometimes
forceful suggestions. In some companies, such as Sony,
the brand champion owns the country brand identities
and positions and takes responsibility for ensuring that

the country teams implement the brand strategy. A brand champion has credibility and respect not only because of organizational power but also because of a depth of experience, knowledge, and insight. A suggestion from a brand champion gets careful consideration.

P&G plans to evolve over the next decade toward a brand champion approach. It believes that it can achieve greater cooperation and create more global brands by concentrating authority and responsibility in the hands of high-level brand champions. At the moment, P&G regards only a handful of its 83 major brands as global.

Most global brand managers have little authority and must create a strategy without the ability to mandate.

GLOBAL BRAND MANAGER

In many companies, particularly in the high-tech and service industries, top management lacks a branding or even a marketing background. The branding expertise rests just below the top line managers. Such companies are often decentralized and have a powerful regional and country line-management system. Effective global brand managers are necessary in these cases to combat local bias and spur unified efforts across countries.

Some global brand managers have sign-off authority for certain marketing programs, but most have little authority. They must attempt to create a global brand strategy without the ability to mandate. There are five keys to success in these situations:

- Companies must have believers at the top; otherwise global brand managers will be preoccupied with convincing the executive suite that brands are worth supporting. If there are no believers, a brand manager can try to create them. The global brand manager for MasterCard did just that by convincing the organization to form a "miniboard" of six board members and nominating one to be its chair. That person became the brand's voice during board meetings.

- A global brand manager needs to either create a planning process or manage an existing one. To make the process effective, all country managers should use the same vocabulary, template, and planning cycle. This is the first step toward fighting local bias.

- A global brand manager should become a key part of the development, management, and operation of an internal brand communication system. By traveling to learn about customers, country managers, problems, and best practices, he or she will be able to maximize the opportunities for cooperation.

- In order to deal with savvy country brand specialists, global brand managers must have global experience, product background, energy, credibility, and people skills. Companies need a system to select, train, mentor, and reward prospects who can fill the role. At Häagen-Dazs, the global brand manager is also the brand manager for the United States, the lead market for its ice cream. The latter position gives the manager credibility because of the resources and knowledge base that come with it.

- Companies can signal the importance of the role through the title they give the manager. At IBM, global brand managers are called brand stewards, a title that reflects the goal of building and protecting brand equity. At Smirnoff, the global brand manager is given the title of president of the Pierre Smirnoff Company, suggesting how much the company values his position.

GLOBAL BRAND TEAM

A global brand manager, acting alone, can be perceived as an outsider—just another corporate staff person contributing to overhead, creating forms, and calling meetings. Sometimes adding people to the mix—in the form of a global brand team—can solve this problem. With a team working on the issue, it becomes easier to convince country brand managers of the value of global brand management.

Global brand teams typically consist of brand representatives from different parts of the world, from different stages of brand development, and from different competitive contexts. Functional areas such as advertising, market research, sponsorship, and promotions may also be represented. The keys to success with these teams are similar to those for the global brand manager.

One problem with a global brand team (unless it is led by a global brand manager) is that no one person ultimately owns the brand globally. Thus no one is responsible for implementing global branding decisions. In addition, team members may be diverted from their task by the pressures of their primary jobs. And the team may lack the authority and focus needed to make sure that their recommendations are actually implemented at the country level. Mobil solves that problem in part by creating "action teams" made up of people from several countries to oversee the implementation.

Some companies partition the global brand manager or team across business units or segments. For example,

Mobil has separate global brand teams for the passenger car lubricant business, the commercial lubricants business, and the fuel business because the brand is fundamentally different in each. A global brand council then coordinates those segments by reconciling the different identities and looking for ways to create brand synergy.

And consider how DuPont handles its Lycra brand. The 35-year-old synthetic is known worldwide for the flexibility and comfort it lends to clothing; its identity is embodied in the global tagline "Nothing moves like Lycra." The problem for Lycra is that it has a variety of applications—it can be used, for example, in swimsuits, in running shorts, and in women's fashions. Each application requires its own brand positioning. DuPont solves the problem by delegating responsibility for each application to managers in a country where that application is strongest. Thus the Brazilian brand manager for Lycra is also the global lead for swimsuit fabric because Brazil is a hotbed for swimsuit design. Similarly, the French brand manager takes the lead for Lycra used in fashion. The idea is to use the expertise that is dispersed throughout the world. The global brand manager for Lycra ensures that those in charge of different applications are together on overall strategy; he or she also pulls together their ideas in order to exploit synergies.

When local management is relatively autonomous, it may be necessary to give the global brand manager or team a significant degree of authority. Doing so can also reduce the chances that the manager or team will get smothered by organizational or competitive pressures; in addition, it can signal the company's commitment to brand building.

Some aspects of the brand's management will be firm, but others will be adaptable or discretionary.

The team or manager may have authority over its visual representation and brand graphics, for example. In that case, the group or the individual would have to approve any departures from the specified color, type-face, and layout of the logo. Or a global brand team may have authority over the look and feel of a product. The IBM ThinkPad is black and rectangular; it has a red tracking ball and a multicolored IBM logo set at 35 degrees in the lower right corner. The global brand team must approve any deviations from that look. In another example, the global brand manager at Smirnoff has sign-off authority on the selection of advertising agencies and themes.

While companies are spelling out the authority of the global brand manager or team, they must also make clear what authority resides with the country team. Some aspects of the brand's management will be firm— the definition of what the brand stands for, say—but others will be adaptable or discretionary, such as the adver-tising presentation or the use of product promotions. The job of the person or group responsible for the brand is to make sure that everyone knows and follows the guidelines.

Delivering Brilliance

Global brand leadership, especially in these days of media clutter, requires real brilliance in brand-building efforts—simply doing a good job isn't enough. The dilemma is how to balance the need to leverage global strengths with the need to recognize local differences. Our research indicates that those who aspire to brilliant execution should do the following:

First, consider what brand-building paths to follow— advertising, sponsorship, increasing retail presence, promotions. The path you choose may turn out to be more important than the way you follow through with it. Experience shows that if the path starts with advertising, as it usually does, other sometimes more innovative and more effective brand-building approaches get the short end of the stick. Second, put pressure on the agency to have the best and most motivated people working on the brand, even if that means creating some agency-client tension. Third, develop options: the more chances at brilliance, the higher the probability that it will be reached. Fourth, measure the results.

P&G finds exceptional ideas by encouraging the country teams to develop breakthrough brand-building programs. Particularly if a brand is struggling, country brand teams are empowered to find a winning formula on their own. Once a winner is found, the organization tests it in other countries and implements it as fast as possible.

For example, when P&G obtained Pantene Pro-V in 1985, it was a brand with a small but loyal following. The company's efforts to expand the product's following in the United States and France did not increase the product's popularity. In 1990, however, brand strategists struck gold in Taiwan. They found that the image of models with shiny healthy hair resonated with Taiwan's consumers. The tagline for the ads was "Hair so healthy it shines." People recognized that they couldn't look just like the models but inside they said, "I've got to have that hair." Within six months, the brand was the leader in Taiwan. The concept and supporting advertising tested well in other markets and was subsequently rolled out in 70 countries.

Another way to stimulate brilliant brand building is to use more than one advertising agency. It's true that a single agency can coordinate a powerful, unified campaign; using only one agency, however, means putting all your creative eggs in one basket. On the other hand, using multiple agencies can lead to inconsistency and strategic anarchy.

In Europe, Audi gets the best of both approaches by following a middle course. It has five agencies from different countries compete to be the lead agency that will create the brand's campaign. The four agencies that lose out are nonetheless retained to implement the winning campaign in their countries. Because the agencies are still involved with Audi, they are available for another round of creative competition in the future. A variant on this approach would be to use several offices from the same agency. That may not lead to as much variation in creative ideas, but it still provides more options than having just one group within one agency.

Adapting global programs to the local level can often improve the effectiveness of a campaign. Take Smirnoff's "pure thrill" vodka campaign. All of its global advertising shows distorted images becoming clear when viewed through the Smirnoff bottle, but the specific scenes change from one country to another in order to appeal to consumers with different assumptions about what is thrilling. In Rio de Janeiro, the ad shows the city's statue of Christ with a soccer ball, and in Hollywood, the "w" in the hillside sign is created with the legs of two people. The IBM global slogan "Solutions for a Small Planet" became "small world" in Argentina where "planet" lacked the desired conceptual thrust.

And yet managers won't be able to tell how well they're building brands unless they develop a global brand measurement system. The system must go beyond financial measures—useful as they are—and measure brand equity in terms of customer awareness, customer loyalty, the brand's personality, and the brand associations that resonate with the public. When these measures of the brand are available, a company has the basis to create programs that will build a strong brand in all markets and to avoid programs that could destroy the brand.

All multinational companies should actively engage in global brand management. Any company that tries to get by with unconnected and directionless local brand strategies will inevitably find mediocrity as its reward. In such cases, an exceptionally talented manager will, on occasion, create a pocket of success. But that success will be isolated and random—hardly a recipe that will produce strong brands around the world.

Originally published in November–December 1999
Reprint 99601

Are the Strategic Stars Aligned for Your Corporate Brand?

MARY JO HATCH AND MAJKEN SCHULTZ

Executive Summary

IN RECENT YEARS, companies have increasingly seen the benefits of creating a corporate brand. Rather than spend marketing dollars on branding individual products, giants like Disney and Microsoft promote a single umbrella image that casts one glow over all their products.

A company must align three interdependent elements—call them strategic stars—to create a strong corporate brand: vision, culture, and image. Aligning the stars takes concentrated managerial skill and will, the authors say, because each element is driven by a different constituency: management, employees, or stakeholders.

To effectively build a corporate brand, executives must identify where their strategic stars fall out of line. The authors offer a series of diagnostic questions designed to reveal misalignments in corporate vision, culture, and image. The first set of questions looks for gaps between vision and culture; for example, when management establishes a vision that is too ambitious for the organization to implement. The second set addresses culture and image, uncovering possible gaps between the attitudes of employees and the perceptions of the outside world. The last set of questions explores the vision-image gap—is management taking the company in a direction that its stakeholders support?

The authors discuss the benefits of a corporate brand, such as reducing marketing costs and building a sense of community among customers. But they also point to cases in which a corporate brand doesn't make sense— for instance, if you are a product incubator, if you've recently experienced M&A activity, or if you are expecting fallout from risky ventures.

WHEN PROCTER & GAMBLE sponsored the Juvenile Diabetes Foundation in New York last year, the company distributed the customary glossy promotional brochure to highlight its generosity. That brochure, however, looked different than those from years past. On the cover, 20 of P&G's flagship products were conspicuously merged in a single symbolic image.

For the granddaddy of product branding, that image may very well reflect a seismic shift in marketing strategy. P&G was founded, after all, on the traditional marketing notion that each product needs a unique identity. Ideally, a brand would grow so strong that, like P&G's own Pampers, it would become a synonym for the product itself.

If the image on the P&G brochure does imply a shift in direction, the company will be joining the ranks of corporate branding giants like Disney, Microsoft, and

Sony. Rather than spend their marketing dollars on branding individual products, those companies promote a corporate brand—a single umbrella image that casts one glow over a panoply of products. In recent years, corporate brands have become enormously valuable assets—companies with strong corporate brands can have market values that are more than twice their book values. (For more on the business case supporting corporate brands, see "What a Corporate Brand Can Do for You" at the end of this article.)

Not surprisingly, creating a corporate brand is both complicated and nuanced. Perhaps that's why so many companies get it wrong. In some cases, an organization will invent a catchy new corporate slogan, tack it on a wide range of products, and hope it will mean something to employees and consumers alike. Just as bad, a company might simply design a new logo and slap it on every product, hoping it will pass as a corporate brand. (See "When a Corporate Brand Doesn't Make Sense" at the end of this article.)

But there is more to it than that. Our research into 100 companies around the world over ten years shows that a company must align three essential, interdependent elements—call them strategic stars—to create a strong corporate brand: vision, culture, and image. As opposed to the shortcuts described above, aligning the stars takes concentrated managerial skill and will. The reason is that a different constituency—management, employees, or stakeholders—drives each element. Consider:

- **Vision:** top management's aspirations for the company.

- **Culture:** the organization's values, behaviors, and attitudes—that is, the way employees all through the ranks feel about the company.

- **Image:** the outside world's overall impression of the company. This includes all stakeholders—customers, shareholders, the media, the general public, and so on.

The Corporate Branding Tool Kit

To effectively build a corporate brand, executives need to identify where their strategic stars fall out of line. To guide managers through this analysis, we have developed the corporate branding tool kit, a series of diagnostic questions designed to reveal misalignments in corporate vision, culture, and image. The first set of questions looks at the relationship between vision and culture; that is, how managers and employees are aligned. The second set addresses culture and image, uncovering possible gaps between the attitudes of employees and the perceptions of the outside world. The last set explores the vision-image gap—is management taking the company in a direction that its stakeholders support?

To get started, take a look at the exhibit "The Corporate Branding Tool Kit." The questions are relatively straightforward, but the investigation itself can be complex and time-consuming. Culling all the relevant information from your top managers, employees, and key stakeholders—through interviews, focus groups, interactive Web sites, and so on—can take months, or even a year or more. Throughout the process, you're trying to detect misalignments between strategic vision, organizational culture, and stakeholder images—even small gaps that might grow into larger ones.

Aligning the elements of your corporate brand is not a sequential process. Vision, culture, and image are intricately interwoven, and you need to conduct the gap analyses concurrently. As you examine the relationship

The Corporate Branding Tool Kit

To get the most out of a corporate branding strategy, three essential elements must be aligned: vision, culture, and image. Aligning these "strategic stars" takes concentrated managerial skill and will. Each element is driven by a different constituency:

• **Vision**
Top management's aspirations for the company.

• **Culture**
The organization's values, behaviors, and attitudes—that is, the way employees all through the ranks feel about the company they are working for.

• **Image**
The outside world's overall impression of the company. This includes all stakeholders—customers, shareholders, the media, the general public, and so on.

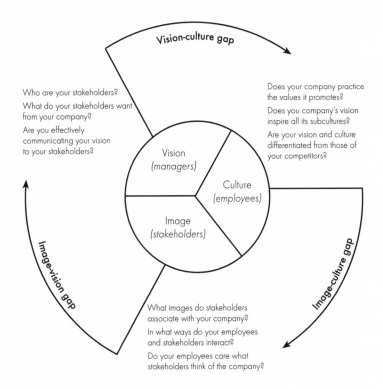

Vision-culture gap

Who are your stakeholders?
What do your stakeholders want from your company?
Are you effectively communicating your vision to your stakeholders?

Does your company practice the values it promotes?
Does you company's vision inspire all its subcultures?
Are your vision and culture differentiated from those of your competitors?

Vision (managers)

Culture (employees)

Image (stakeholders)

Image-vision gap

Image-culture gap

What images do stakeholders associate with your company?
In what ways do your employees and stakeholders interact?
Do your employees care what stakeholders think of the company?

between, say, vision and image or image and culture, there will be some overlap. Don't worry. This is the natural result of the interdependence of the elements.

The tool is useful in identifying the key problem areas—the vision-culture gap, the image-culture gap, and the image-vision gap—but the hard work of developing specific solutions and implementing them belongs to you and your team.

THE VISION-CULTURE GAP

This misalignment develops when senior management moves the company in a strategic direction that employees don't understand or support. The gap usually emerges when senior management establishes a vision that is too ambitious for the organization to implement. The main symptom: a breach between rhetoric and reality. Disappointed managers often blame employees for resisting change; frustrated employees react with cynicism and suspicion. Such scapegoating and distrust are extremely dangerous for companies. Like an ulcer, they can eat away at a corporate brand from within. To uncover possible gaps between vision and culture, managers should ask the following questions of themselves and their employees:

Does your company practice the values it promotes? We all laugh at Dilbert cartoons. But a company where every cubicle is festooned with them is probably in deep trouble. The cartoons use cynical humor to point out the discrepancies between the values a company espouses and those that its systems promote. This isn't a laughing matter. During John Akers's reign at IBM, for example, a joke circulated throughout the company that "IBM means I've been misled." The severe downsizing that took place in the early 1990s in spite of the company's promises of lifelong employment had generated anxiety, depression, and fear among its employees. Needless to say, the effect of such disillusionment on IBM's brand at the time was devastating.

Does your company's vision inspire all its subcultures? Any company, large or small, is made up of subcultures. The engineers in your R&D department will have a different set of values and priorities than those held by the sales and marketing department. Top managers need to be sure that the vision that inspires them—they, too, have a subculture—will resonate throughout the company. A vision that speaks only to the R&D staff will not inspire a company that is dependent on salespeople. The key is to understand what organizational values are shared across the company. Successful corporate visions pick up on those shared values. Bang & Olufsen, the Danish audiovisual company known for its distinctive product designs, for instance, unifies its disparate workforce around a Bauhaus-inspired tradition of simplicity.

Are your vision and culture sufficiently differentiated from those of your competitors? Your vision and culture are your signature. Together, they are a powerful tool in helping you stand out from your competition. Apple is a classic example of a company that successfully differentiated its vision through its unique culture. Thanks to Steve Jobs, Apple saw the potential of computers to change people's everyday lives. Jobs's insight and enthusiasm attracted to Silicon Valley legions of young people who equated Apple with a new way of life. These computer enthusiasts not only created a culture that supported Apple as it grew but also altered the shape of the computer industry forever.

THE IMAGE-CULTURE GAP

Misalignment between a company's image and organizational culture leads to confusion among customers about what a company stands for. This usually means that a company doesn't practice what it preaches, so its image gets tarnished among key stakeholders. In today's wired world, where word-of-mouth opinion spreads through Internet chat rooms as quickly as the flu through a kindergarten, maintaining a positive image is increasingly challenging. To identify image-culture gaps, you need to compare what your employees are saying with what your customers and other stakeholders are saying.

What images do stakeholders associate with your company? The first step in uncovering an image-culture gap is to understand the images that outsiders have of you. These images are both real and perceived—they stem as much from an individual's feelings, thoughts, and opinions as from the facts of your company. They can be startlingly different, therefore, from the image that the company seeks to project. And when stakeholders find that the culture of an organization does not match their subjective image, it often spells disaster for the company. Consider British Airways. When it decided to go global, BA launched a campaign to change the image of the airline. The company used advertising to persuade the public to view BA as a global airline; "the world's *favorite* airline" was now "the *world's* favorite airline." To communicate its new image, BA repainted the tail fins of its aircraft with artwork from around the world. Unfortunately, the prim uniforms of the cabin crew and the silver tea service continued to give passengers the impression that BA was distinctly British. Caught in the chasm between image and culture, BA's branding experiment failed.

In what ways do your employees and stakeholders interact? The next line of questioning focuses on the channels through which a company reaches out to stakeholders. While advertising and public relations can counter negative images, nothing is more powerful than stakeholders' direct, personal encounters with the organization. Energy giant Shell, for example, not only listens to its customers but also seeks feedback from investors, community members, and activists through focus groups, surveys, and its Web-based "Tell-Shell" program. Unfortunately, many companies put obstacles in the way of such communications, to the detriment of their corporate brands. Consider the potential for misalignment when marketing talks to customers, HR talks to employees, public relations talks to the media, but the departments don't talk to one another.

Do your employees care what stakeholders think of the company? An inauthentic organizational culture can jeopardize a corporate brand. Take Coca-Cola, which used to have one of the world's most powerful corporate brands. Recent events—including the distribution of tainted beverages in Belgium and alleged profiteering among distributors—have led to a gap between the company's culture and image. How could the employees of the company that "taught the world to sing" be a party to the exploitation of its customers? This fundamental misalignment has tarnished the image of Coca-Cola. The company must now work to correct the deterioration in its culture that led to the scandals.

THE IMAGE-VISION GAP

The third obstacle for creating an effective corporate brand is conflict between outsiders' images and management's strategic vision. Companies cannot afford to ignore their stakeholders; the most carefully crafted strategic visions will fail if they are not aligned with what customers want from the company. Having sounded out employees and stakeholders, managers need to find out whether they are out of sync themselves.

Who are your stakeholders? Managers who ask themselves this seemingly obvious question are frequently surprised by what they learn. For example, many companies find that their products reach a very different market from the ones they are targeting. Consider Nike in the mid-1980s. At the time, the company saw itself as a high-performance athletic-shoe manufacturer that attended only to the needs of top athletes. But market research later showed that more than half of Nike's sales were going to people who were wearing the athletic footwear as a substitute for casual shoes. This image-vision misalignment meant that Nike was not capitalizing on an important market.

What do your stakeholders want from your company? Just as there can be a disconnect between a company's culture and its image, so too is there frequently a gap between management's vision and the images and expectations customers have for a company. After Nike discovered that its products were being sold as substitutes for casual shoes, for example, it produced a line of conventional casual shoes—that nobody wanted. Consumers wanted the same shoes their athletic heroes were wearing. Before the company could exploit what was obviously a hot market, Nike had to come to grips with the fact that it didn't matter that the sneakers were over-engineered for the average customer. The appeal was in the image of athleticism that the sneakers projected.

Are you effectively communicating your vision to your stakeholders? Marshall McLuhan memorably said the medium is the message. Though we wouldn't go that far, we have no doubt that many companies underestimate the importance of the way they communicate their vision to outsiders. Having created an inspiring vision backed up with cultural values, corporate managers all too often fail to check their work with their stakeholders. Recall British Airways. Once it had privatized, BA decided it was time to fully globalize its brand. In addition to repainting the planes' tail fins, the company decided to remove the British flag from all its aircraft. The British press went ballistic. A cabin-crew strike broke out. Business-class travelers threatened to switch allegiance. This time a gap had developed between BA's vision and its image, and executives were forced to acknowledge they had gotten it wrong again, and they abandoned the program. BA finally got the message—it was a public icon that could not afford to ignore its stakeholders.

The corporate brand tool kit will not by itself identify all the problems you are likely to have with your corporate brand. But it does provide a useful framework for reality testing and will help you uncover the most obvious gaps. You should tailor the questions to your company and drill deeper in areas of particular concern. It's also helpful to compare responses from different constituencies to similar questions. For example, you can compare how managers, employees, and stakeholders rate the way the company communicates its vision. A lack of consensus between the groups—or worse, among members of the same group—will signal an important disconnect.

Getting the Stars Lined Up

Using a process like the corporate brand tool kit can help companies get the most from their corporate brands.

That's what happened at Lego, the fourth largest toy-maker in the world. For years, the company's top managers recognized that Lego's most valuable asset was its image as a producer of imaginative and inventive construction toys. But in the mid-1990s, the market for the toys started to decline, and Lego managers knew they had to reinvent the company. Its image was an obvious place to start.

How did Lego go about building on its image? The first step was to find out exactly what images stakeholders had of the company and its products. Lego turned to outside experts such as Young & Rubicam, a leading advertising agency, for a global assessment of its image. They found that, in the minds of its stakeholders, Lego's image was as strong as those of some of the world's most powerful players, such as Disney and Microsoft. The revelation encouraged Lego executives to stop thinking of the company in terms of products—the celebrated Lego bricks—and dare to see themselves as leaders in the business of creativity and learning.

The next step in developing the corporate brand was to bring vision in line with image. This was done by holding brainstorming sessions for top managers and people outside Lego—academics in business strategy and child development as well as dedicated customers—who had long-standing relationships with the company. Lego executives deliberately searched for a vision that would inspire the whole organizational culture as well as customers and other stakeholders. The result was a catchy new slogan—"just imagine..."—and a bold new vision statement. Lego vowed to become the strongest brand among families with children by 2005. Company owner and president Kjeld Kirk Kristiansen held companywide seminars to launch the new vision. The process was

inspirational. Lego got the guidance and input it needed
to create a powerful new corporate vision that was in
keeping with the company's image: imagination, invention, togetherness, learning, and, of course, fun.

But aligning two of the three stars wasn't enough.
Lego also needed an organizational culture that could
support the vision and give the images credibility. That's
why it invited managers and employees from all over the
world to participate in "pit stops." At these workshops,
which have so far involved some 7,000 employees, individuals share their dreams for the company and themselves, building support for the brand in the process. In
addition, the company organizes "dream-outs," similar
to GE's workouts, where employees participate in interactive, real-time problem solving. One dream-out
improved distribution channels in the United States,
another found new ways of responding to customer
needs for their infants. Pit stops and dream-outs are
activities that align Lego's culture behind the vision, and
together they have transformed the employee mind-set
from toy producers to brand warriors.

Of course, even though it took exceptional care to
align image, vision, and culture, Lego faced lingering ten-
sions when it moved to roll out the corporate brand. A
few product brand managers resisted the corporate
brand and had to be let go. The company itself had to
reorganize. But the transformation at Lego was well
worth the effort. According to Lego's 1999 annual report,
the benefits of the corporate brand strategy and the
investments in new business ideas and people development had already started to show in the 28% increase in
the company's global net sales. Last year, the Lego brick
was named toy of the century by *Fortune* magazine. The
company grabbed more honors when it received the "Toy

of the Century" award from the British Association of Toy Retailers for its classic Lego bricks and its ability to create new inventions such as Mindstorms.

While corporate vision and culture are themselves powerful strategic tools, once they are aligned with stakeholder images, the corporate brand can become a powerhouse.

By identifying all elements of the corporate brand—and by exposing any gaps in their interaction—the corporate branding tool kit can help companies reap the benefits of a corporate branding strategy. The tool eliminates much of the ambiguity involved in creating and maintaining a corporate brand. As a result, managers can take charge of those brands and use the strategic stars as competitive weapons.

What a Corporate Brand Can Do for You

CREATING A CORPORATE BRAND—an umbrella image that casts one glow over an array of products—is a relatively new approach to integrating a company's stakeholders. With the notable exceptions we have mentioned, most major companies, like P&G, have been better known for their product brands than for their corporate brands. But an increasing number of companies are discovering just how much value there is in a strong corporate brand.

Corporate Brands Reduce Costs

U.S. companies together can save billions of dollars by using corporate brands to exploit economies of scale in advertising and marketing. SmithKline Beecham, for example, now uses its corporate brand to support all its products. Corporate brands make good sense for companies that compete in markets where product life cycles have shortened, making it difficult to recover the costs of continually creating new product brands. Nestlé and Unilever are moving in this direction, each reducing the number of product brands they market.

They Give Customers a Sense of Community

Many customers are willing to pay more for some badge of identification–say, Apple's rainbow-colored logo–that makes them feel they are part of a community. Another notable example is Virgin. Across the company's diverse businesses–airlines, megastores, cola, and mobile phones–Virgin's top management, led by flamboyant CEO Richard Branson, has meticulously cultivated the distinctive positioning of David versus Goliath: "We're on your side against the fat cats." This has led to the widespread perception that Virgin is a company with a distinctive personality: innovative, challenging, fun.

They Provide a Seal of Approval

A strong corporate brand lets customers know what they can expect of the whole range of products that a company produces. Take Sony, for example. Its corporate logo of four block letters, whether applied to a stereo, a television, or a computer game, stands for the high level of competence, quality, and care for detail shared by all the products that are sold under the Sony name. A strong corporate brand also helps a company defend itself against outside assault. Consider the Body Shop. When a journalist recently accused the company of lacking integrity in its testing of beauty products, the company overtly appealed to the public by citing its corporate brand, which was firmly associated in people's minds with strong ethical standards concerning animal rights.

They Create Common Ground

The most successful corporate brands are universal and so paradoxically facilitate differences of interpretation that appeal to different groups. This is particularly true of corporate brands whose symbolism is robust enough to allow people across cultures to share symbols even when they don't share the same meaning. A good example is the McDonald's golden arches. One of the most powerful corporate brands ever created, the golden arches resonate in the hearts and minds of people all over the world—even though different cultures attach different meanings to them. McDonald's promotes and supports these differences of interpretation, breathing life into its corporate brand around the world.

When a Corporate Brand Doesn't Make Sense

ESTÉE LAUDER HAS A STRONG corporate brand, but the company is driven by a number of product brands, such as Origins and Mac. The Gap has three successful product brands—Banana Republic, Old Navy, and the Gap—but many customers are unaware that they're all part of the same company. Are these companies lagging behind the times? Not necessarily. Sometimes product brands just make more sense, especially:

If You Are a Product Incubator

If your company's mission is to create and then sell off successful product brands, imposing a corporate brand on them doesn't make sense. For example, many biotechnology and information technology companies make significant profits selling spin-off companies. This was the case, for example, when Danish NKT sold its subsidiary, Giga, to Intel for more than $1 billion. Because NKT's business model is based on selling off other companies in the future, it holds them under separate names. In such cases, overt corporate branding could detract from the selling price if the potential buyers believed that disassociating the unit from its current owner's brand would be costly.

After M&A Activity

In industries such as finance and telecommunications, where frequent international mergers and acquisitions can affect stakeholder comfort, many companies will choose to preserve their national brands. Take the case of banking. After a bank is acquired, customer trust and loyalty are unlikely to be transferred automatically to the new bank owners. That's why Scandinavia's largest financial company, Nordic Baltic Holding, maintains local brands such as MeritaNordbanken in Sweden and Finland, Unibank in Denmark, and Christiania Bank in Norway. Maintaining national brand names, at least in the short term, can help ease the turmoil of changing ownership.

If You Are Expecting Fallout

Firms that like to take risks in new markets might not want to bet their corporate brands by associating them with untried products—unless the corporate brand, like

Virgin's, is associated with high-risk ventures. Also, in industries like oil or chemicals where practices can raise ethical concerns or companies face repeated crises or scandals, the downside of corporate branding can be steep. Any negative publicity associated with the company will spill over onto all the products it labels with its name or associates with its official symbols.

Originally published in February 2001
Reprint R0102K

Torment Your Customers (They'll Love It)

STEPHEN BROWN

Executive Summary

IN THE PAST DECADE, marketing gurus have called for customer care, customer focus, even–shudder–customer centricity. But according to marketing professor Stephen Brown, the customer craze has gone too far. In this article, he makes the case for "retromarketing"–a return to the days when marketing succeeded by tormenting customers rather than pandering to them. Using vivid examples, Brown shows that many recent consumer marketing coups have decidedly not been customer-driven. They've relied instead on five basic retromarketing principles:

Exclusivity. Retromarketing eschews the modern marketing proposition of "here it is, there's plenty for everyone" by holding back supplies and delaying gratification. You want it? Can't have it. Try again later, pal.

Secrecy. Whereas modern marketing is up-front and transparent, retromarketing revels in mystery, intrigue, and covert operations. (Consider the classic "secret" recipes that have helped to purvey all sorts of comestibles.) The key is to make sure the existence of a secret is never kept secret.

Amplification. In a world of incessant commercial chatter, amplification is vital, and it can be induced in many ways, from mystery to affront to surprise.

Entertainment. Marketing must divert, engage, and amuse. The lack of entertainment is modern marketing's greatest failure.

Tricksterism. Customers loved to be teased. The tricks don't have to be elaborate to be effective; they can come cheap. But the rewards can be great if the brand is embraced, even briefly, by the in crowd.

Managers may be dismayed by the thought of deliberately thwarting consumers. But if markets were *really* customer oriented, they'd give their customers what they want: old-style, gratuitously provocative marketing.

Don't get me wrong: I have nothing against customers. Some of my best friends are customers. Customers are a good thing, by and large, provided they're kept well downwind.

My problem is with the concept of—and I shudder to write the term—"customer centricity." Everyone in business today seems to take it as a God-given truth that companies were put on this earth for one purpose alone: to pander to customers. Marketers spend all their time slavishly tracking the needs of buyers, then meticulously crafting products and pitches to satisfy them. If corporate functions were Dickens characters, marketing would be Uriah Heep: unctuous, ubiquitous, unbearable.

My friends, it's gone too far.

The truth is, customers don't know what they want. They never have. They never will. The wretches don't even know what they *don't* want, as the success of countless rejected-by-focus-groups products, from the Chrysler minivan to the Sony Walkman, readily attests. A mindless devotion to customers means me-too products, copycat advertising campaigns, and marketplace stagnation.

And customers don't really want to be catered to, anyway. I've spent most of my career studying marketing campaigns, and my research shows that many of the marketing coups of recent years have been far from customer centric. Or at least, the successes have proceeded from a deeper understanding of what people want than would ever emerge from the bowels of a data mine. Whatever people may desire of their products and services, they adamantly do not want kowtowing from the companies that market to them. They do not want us to prostrate ourselves in front of them and promise to love them, till death us do part. They'd much rather be teased, tantalized, and tormented by deliciously insatiable desire.

It's time to get back to an earlier marketing era, to the time when marketers ruled the world with creativity and style. It's time to break out the snake oil again. It's time for retromarketing.

Retro Shock

Retromarketing is based on an eternal truth: Marketers, like maidens, get more by playing hard to get. That's the antithesis of what passes for modern marketing. These days, marketers aim to make life simple for the consumer by getting goods to market in a timely and efficient manner, so that they are available when and where they're wanted, at a price people are prepared to pay. Could anything be more boring? By contrast, retromarketing makes 'em work for it, by limiting availability, by delaying gratification, by heightening expectations, by fostering an enigmatic air of unattainability. It doesn't serve demand; it creates it.

As marketing strategies go, "Don't call us, we'll call you" is about as far from today's customer-hugging norm as it is possible to imagine. But it suits the times. We are, after all, in the midst of a full-blown nostalgia boom, a fact not lost on most successful product designers and advertisers. Retro is everywhere, whether it be Camel Lite's series of pseudonostalgic posters (a leather-helmeted flying ace lights up with a Zippo); Keds's television commercial for its old-style sneakers (reengineered, naturally, for today's demanding consumers); the McDonald's rollout of retrofitted diners (which offer table service and 1950s favorites like mashed potatoes and gravy); Disney's Celebration, a new olde town in Florida, just like the ones that never existed (outside of Hollywood studio back lots); or Restoration Hardware, a nationwide retail chain selling updated replicas of old-fashioned fixtures, fittings, and furnishings (perfect for redecorating that Rockwellian colonial in Celebration). Retro chic is de rigueur in everything from cameras, coffeepots, and radios to toasters, telephones, and refrigerators. Retro roller coasters, steam trains, airships, motorbikes, and ballparks are proliferating, as are reproductions of sports equipment from earlier days. Tiki bars are back; polyester jumpsuits are cavorting on the catwalks; shag carpet is getting laid in the most tasteful abodes; and retro autos, such as the PT Cruiser and the new T-Bird, are turning heads all around the country. It's reached the point, comedian George Carlin says, where we don't experience déjà vu, but vujà dé—those rare moments when we have an uncanny sense that what we're experiencing has *never happened before.*

People aren't just suckers for old-fashioned goods and services, they also yearn for the marketing of times gone by. They actually miss the days when a transaction was just a transaction, when purchasing a bar of soap didn't mean entering into a life-time value relationship. Wary of CRM-inspired tactics, which are tantamount to stalking, they appreciate the true transparency of a blatant huckster. Retro-marketing recognizes that today's consumer is nothing if not marketing savvy. Call it postmodern, but people enjoy the ironic art of a well-crafted sales pitch. The best of retromarketing hits consumers with the hardest of sells, all the while letting them in on the joke. (See "Time for a New Motown Revival" at the end of this article.)

Retromarketing eschews the modern marketing proposition by deliberately holding back supplies. You want it? Can't have it. Try again later, pal.

Going Retro

Just like retrostyling, retromarketing is more art than science. It's easy to hit a false note. But can its lessons be spelled out? Is there an ABC for wannabes? They can, and there is. And although arrogant academicians always advocate acronyms, aphorisms, apothegms, and absurdly affected alliterations—to ensure ever-busy executives *get it*—retromarketing represents a rare renunciation of this ridiculous rhetorical rule. There are just five basic principles.

The first is that customers crave *exclusivity*. Retro-marketing eschews the "here it is, come and get it, there's plenty for everyone" proposition—the modern market-ing proposition—by deliberately holding back supplies and delaying gratification. You want it? Can't have it. Try again later, pal.

Granted, "Get it now while supplies last" is one of the oldest arrows in the marketing quiver. But it is no less effective for all that. First, exclusivity helps you avoid excess inventory—you don't make it until the customer begs for it. Second, it allows buyers to luxuriate in the belief that they are the lucky ones, the select few, the dis-cerning elite. Promoting exclusivity is standard practice in the motor industry, as would-be buyers of Miatas, Harleys, and Honda Odysseys will readily testify. It's employed by De Beers for diamonds and Disney for videos. It's used by everyone from Wall Street brokers, with an IPO to pass off, to the chocolate conspirators at Cadbury, whose creme eggs are strictly rationed and highly seasonal. Indeed, it has launched countless one-day, 13-hour, blue-light, everything-must-go sales in retail stores the world over, and doubtless it will con-tinue to do so.

Ty Warner, impresario of toy maker Ty Incorporated, may well go down in history for his ceaselessly inventive exploitation of exclusivity. To be sure, his velveteen storm troopers—the famous Beanie Babies—looked like undernourished attendees at the teddy bears' picnic. Nevertheless, their retromarketing campaign put Sun Tzu's *The Art of War* to shame. By coupling limited pro-duction runs with ruthless "retirements," Warner ensured that Beanie Babies remained in enormous demand and fostered a now-or-never mind-set among consumers and retailers.

Ostensibly priced at five or six bucks apiece, Beanies fetched upwards of three grand at auction and were known to trigger fistfights among frenzied I-spotted-it-first fans. They were sold through a plethora of small-time gift shops, bypassing major retail chains, whose EDI-driven ethos of regular supplies, no surprises, and guaranteed delivery times was anathema to Warner. Consistently inconsistent, he supplied what he wanted, when he wanted, to whomsoever he wanted, and if the retailers didn't like it, then they simply did without. When added to the constant introductions and retirements of models, the upshot was that Warner's wares were scattered hither and yon. Reason didn't enter into it, let alone rhyme. The tush-tagged creatures could thus be discovered in the most out-of-the-way outlets, which added to rather than detracted from Beanies' pseudo-nostalgic appeal. Fuelled, furthermore, by a massive word-of-mouse rumor mill, as well as an enormous secondary market in collectibles, Ty Warner turned the ultimate trick of making brand-new, mass-produced toys into semiprecious "antiques."

"Expect the unexpected" was Ty's rallying cry, and most would agree that capricious production, idiosyncratic distribution, eccentric promotion, and haphazard pricing are somewhat unusual in a modern marketing world of Analysis, Planning, Implementation, and Control. However, it is very much in keeping with a premodern milieu of restricted supply, excess demand, and multifarious channels of distribution. As Warner sagely observed, "As long as kids keep fighting over the products and retailers are angry at us because they cannot get enough, I think those are good signs." Indeed, the fighting would have continued had Warner not ultimately betrayed his own best retromarketing instincts. After deciding to terminate Beanie Babies en masse in December 1999, he was persuaded by an on-line plebiscite to grant a soft-toy stay of execution. Collectors were not amused, and Warner's iconic standing suffered irreparable damage.

Happily, right on Ty's heels came another tour de force of customer torment from the master marketers behind today's greatest mania: Harry Potter. Not only is J.K. Rowling's remarkable creation the perfect retro product—a twenty-first-century Tom Brown—but the wonderful wizard of Hogwarts has been marketed in an unashamedly retro manner. Scholastic's campaign for the blockbuster *Harry Potter and the Goblet of Fire* is a sterling example of the second principle of retromarketing: *secrecy*. It consisted of a complete blackout on advance information. The book's title, pagination, and price were kept under wraps until two weeks before publication. Review copies were withheld, no author interviews were allowed, and foreign translations were deferred for fear of injudicious leaks. Juicy plot details, including the death of a key character and Harry's sexual awakening, were drip fed to a slavering press corps prior to the launch. Printers and distributors were required to sign strict confidentiality agreements. Booksellers were bound by a ruthlessly policed embargo, though some were allowed to display the tantalizing volume in locked cages for a brief period just before "Harry Potter Day," July 8, 2000. And in a stroke of retro genius, several advance copies were "accidentally" sold from an unnamed Wal-Mart in deepest West Virginia, though one of the "lucky" children was miraculously tracked down by the world's press and splashed across every front page worth its salt.

More sadistic still, Scholastic dropped less-than-subtle hints that there weren't enough copies of the book to go around, thereby exacerbating the gotta-get-it frenzy of fans and distributors alike. In the event, the tome was ubiquitously unavoidable, available everywhere from grocery stores to roadside restaurants. No one complained, of course, because everyone had managed to get their hands on the precious Potter, and by the time they'd finished reading the magical mystery, they'd forgotten its magically mysterious marketing campaign. Now you see it, now you don't.

Whereas modern marketing is upfront, above board, and transparent, retro revels in mystery, intrigue, and covert operations. Consider the classic "secret" recipes that have helped to purvey all sorts of comestibles—Coca-Cola, Heinz Ketchup, Kentucky Fried Chicken, Mrs. Fields Cookies, the list goes on—to say nothing of cosmetics (the secret of youthfulness), proprietary medicines (the secret of good health), and holiday packages (secret hideaways a specialty). If it engages the customer in even just a moment of consideration of the product—"What could it be?" or simply, "Why is it so hush-hush?"—secrecy helps to sell.

But what, you may well ask, is the secret of successful secrecy? Obviously, it's that the existence of a secret must never be kept secret. There's no point in having an exclusive product or service unless everyone who is anyone knows about it. But when big-budget marketing campaigns are unaffordable or inappropriate, what's a brand to do? The answer,

There's nothing like a little outrage to attract attention and turn a tiny advertising spend into a megabudget monster.

and the third principle of retromarketing, is to *amplify*—that is, to ensure that the hot ticket or cool item is talked about and, more important, that the talking about is talked about.

The power of amplification can be seen in the recent buzz about "Ginger," the mysterious and much-talked-about creation by Dean Kamen. Widely regarded as the heir apparent to Thomas Edison, Kamen is a throwback to the amateur inventor archetype, a garage-based, gizmo-surrounded, patent-collecting tinkerer. He made his name—and his millions—with a portable insulin pump, a suitcase-sized dialysis machine, and, most recently, a gyroscopic, stair-climbing wheelchair. And now he has created Ginger, the code name for what is allegedly the greatest invention since the sliced bread cliché. The Net-propelled speculation surrounding the invention, known simply as "IT," has been overwhelming. Starved for actual information about the invention, the media has scrambled to report on the reports of the media. In the process, Ginger's become famous for being famous, as historian Daniel Boorstin famously put it—and marketed for being unmarketed. To date, no one knows what IT is exactly, and the seer's not saying. All we know for certain is that IT is so revolutionary that entire cities will be retrofitted to accommodate IT. Seal off those sidewalks. Rip up those autoroutes. Tear down those tollbooths. Ginger's coming down the turnpike, powered by a perpetual-motion motor that runs on hot air and hyperbole. Surprisingly, no one seems to have noticed the echoes in this craze of a classic P.T. Barnum marketing caper of 1860. Barnum's "it" turned out to be an encephalitic giantess from New Jersey; Kamen, it seems, simply plans to encephalize the New Jersey expressways. Clearly, they're being born at more than one a minute these days.

In a world of incessant commercial chatter, amplification is vitally necessary, and it can be induced in many ways beyond just mystery. One of the most cost-effective techniques is affront. Whether it be Calvin Klein, Benetton, or even Citroën—its Picasso minivan tweaked French aesthetes by appropriating the master's moniker—there's nothing like a little outrage to attract attention and turn a tiny advertising spend into a megabudget monster. Better yet, it bestows an aura of attractive insouciance on the I-fought-the-law offenders.

Another powerful amplifier is surprise. An unexpected marketing campaign can send shock waves through the media—as when Pizza Hut paid to have its logo placed on the side of a Russian rocket, or when Taco Bell offered a free taco to everyone in the United States if the decommissioned Mir managed to hit a 40-by-40-foot floating target placed at the anticipated splashdown site.

So much the better if all this marketing is *entertaining,* which brings us to principle number four of retromarketing: Marketing must divert. It must engage. It must amuse. Entertainment, in many ways, is the essence of retromarketing—and the lack of it is modern marketing's greatest failure.

I blame my esteemed colleague Philip Kotler, the renowned Northwestern University marketing professor, for this sorry state of affairs. He, more than anyone, has convinced managers that marketing is the backbone of business and must integrate the work of all other functions. Weighed down by this awesome responsibility, marketing has become a sober-sided discipline. It has lost its sense of fun. It has forgotten how to flirt.

The marketers of Hollywood, not surprisingly, have been resolute holdouts—not least in their latter-day use of the Internet. The Web site to promote the recent remake of *Planet of the Apes,* for example, contains an elaborate treasure hunt. *Swordfish*'s site offers a $100,000 prize to anyone who can crack ten passwords.

Most ambitious of all is the Web-based promotion of
Steven Spielberg's *AI,* which premiered in June 2001. It's
a surreptitious campaign, designed to be discovered
and passed on from one cool person to another. Like
the old record producer's trick of planting hidden messages between tracks (remember "I buried Paul"?), the
process begins with a fake name inserted into the cred-
its of a trailer for the movie. A Web search on that
name leads the curious to a series of planted Web sites,
a discovery of a murder, and a growing body of clues.
Before long, cryptic e-mails and spooky phone messages
come into play—and those who have followed the
thread to that point are embroiled in a story quite separate from the film. Clearly, the marketers involved—
highly aware that a movie lives or dies on its first two
weeks of word of mouth—engineered a way to generate
that buzz just before *AI* premiered. And it's more creative than concocting fake columnists or planting vox-
pop puffery.

The *AI* campaign also exemplifies the final principle
of retromarketing: marketing must deal in *tricksterism,*
using tactics akin to those of Loki (of Norse myth), the
wily Coyote (of Native American legend), and Hermes
(the Greek god of the marketplace). The tricks don't have
to be particularly elaborate; on the contrary, tricks can
come cheap, as the now classic *Blair Witch Project*—is it
a snuff movie or not?—bears eloquent witness. Similarly,
the recent turn to sneaky sales promotions, where, for
instance, the gregarious, round-buying barfly in the way-
cool club is actually an employee of a liquor company,
involves minimal expenditure on the marketer's part.
However, the rewards can be great if the brand is
embraced, even briefly, by the in-crowd.

A particularly sly bit of tricksterism was served up by the makers of Tango, a fruit juice soda popular in the United Kingdom. In 1994, the company bought advertising time and used it for what appeared to be a public service announcement; its "marketing director" warned viewers that some rogue supermarkets and convenience stores were selling a knockoff of the brand—it could be detected because it was not fizzy—and asked them to report the miscreant outlets by calling a special, toll-free hot line. Apparently, some 30,000 people rang up, only to be informed that they had been tricked ("Tango'd") as part of the company's promotion for a new, noncarbonated version of the drink. The ITC—Britain's TV-advertising watchdog—was not amused, and it rapped Tango's knuckles for abusing the public-information service format. In the meantime, the promotion had succeeded in amplifying the product launch and adding to Tango's incorrigibly irreverent image.

Being a trickster is not the same as being a downright cheater. Cheating, to state the obvious, is wrong, and people won't stand for it. The charlatanry I'm advocating comes with an extra dimension of panache, of exaggeration, of sheer chutzpah, which renders the unacceptable acceptable. Modern marketers set great store by the truth, and one can understand why, given marketing's less-than-illustrious heritage of diddling, double-dealing, and deceit. The truth, however, is that people don't want the truth, the whole truth, and nothing but

Marketing managers have fallen for their own line. They actually believe that if you love the customer enough, the customer will love you back. That is complete nonsense.

the truth. And even if they did, the last place they'd look for it would be a marketing campaign. Marketing is about glitz and glamour. It's mischievous and mysterious. Marketing, lest we forget, is fun.

From Four P's to Pure Tease

Retromarketing, then, is based on *exclusivity*, *secrecy*, *amplification*, *entertainment*, and *tricksterism*. At least this list of principles doesn't create an acronym...unless, of course, the sequence is reversed. To be sure, retromarketing is not appropriate on every occasion, nor is it applicable to every product, service, or market segment. But, then, the modern marketing concept of caring, sharing, all hold hands is not always the right approach, either.

Marketing managers, admittedly, may be dismayed by the thought of deliberately thwarting consumers. That's because they've fallen for their own line. They actually believe that if you love the customer enough, the customer will love you back. That is complete nonsense. Consumers, as a rule, don't love or care for marketing types, especially when they purport to have the customers' interests at heart. Consumers *want* to dislike marketers, they *like* to dislike marketers, they *need* someone to hate, particularly in politically correct times when ethnic stereotyping and other such nastiness is effectively forbidden. Contemporary consumers are embarrassed by marketers who get down on one knee and promise to love, honor, and obey. Get real! They would much prefer a good old-fashioned lovable rogue. Indeed, if marketers were *really* customer oriented, they'd give their customers what they want. Namely, old-style, gratuitously provocative marketing rather than the neutered, defanged, Disneyfied version that's peddled today.

Retromarketing, in sum, harks back to the good old bad old days when marketers were pranksters and proud of it. It replaces the Seven S's with seven veils. Its Five Forces are flim, flam, flirt, fiddle, and finagle. Its Four P's are perturb, puzzle, perplex, and perhaps. Its Three C's are chafe, chide, and chortle. It puts the mark into marketing, the con into concept, the cuss into customers. It's a marketing philosophy for a retro-besotted world. It's tried and true. It's the greatest show on earth.

Would I lie to you?

Time for a New Motown Revival

OF ALL INDUSTRIES, the automotive business is most responsible for perfecting the art of retro. It invented the Joe Isuzu–style salesman and has been quick to tap into nostalgic yearnings in its new model designs and advertising. How sad, then, to see the industry suppressing its true nature and embracing customer centricity as its marketing approach.

Just consider its retro credentials. The Mazda Miata, an homage to 1950s roadsters, which comes complete with a carefully pitched tailpipe note, was the first retro auto rollout. Its triumph in the marketplace set the entire motor industry on the road to yesterville. Fast followers include the Chrysler PT Cruiser, a pastiche of the upright sedans of the 1940s; the Jaguar S-Type, an affectionate nod to the style of the immortal Mark II, beloved by British police officers and their criminal counterparts; and, best of all, the New Beetle, which melds the distinctive shape of the old Beetle with the latest automotive technology to produce a modern car with anachronistic styling. Not to be outdone, the retro auto prototype, Mazda's Miata, recently celebrated its decade-long heritage with a tenth anniversary special edition, thus making it a neo retro auto.

Yet despite the success of the retro products, the automobile industry hasn't fully embraced retromarketing. For every old-style publicity stunt, there are dozens of oleaginous allusions to market responsiveness, customer care, and our duty is to serve. Saturn says it all.

Auto marketers are unnecessarily ashamed of their Artful Dodger antecedents. They try to hide inveigling away, to disguise their deceitful DNA, only to suffer from the return of retromarketing repressed. It's time for the madness to end. The return of Joe Isuzu is a start, but the therapy must go deeper. It's time, carmakers, to get in touch with your inner huckster.

Originally published in October 2001
Reprint R0109E

Boost Your Marketing ROI with Experimental Design

ERIC ALMQUIST AND GORDON WYNER

Executive Summary

CONSUMERS ARE REGULARLY BLITZED with thousands of marketing messages—television commercials, telephone solicitations, supermarket circulars, and Internet banner ads. Still, a lot of these messages fail to hit their targets or elicit the desired response: the purchase of a product or service. It has been very difficult for companies to isolate what drives consumer behavior, largely because there are so many possible combinations of stimuli.

In this article, consultants Eric Almquist and Gordon Wyner explain that while marketing has always been a creative endeavor, adopting a scientific approach to it may actually make it easier—and more cost effective—for companies to target the right customers. "Experimental design" techniques, which have long been applied in other fields, let people project the impact of many stimuli by testing just a few of them. By using mathematical formulas to select and test a subset of combinations of variables, marketers can model hundreds or even thousands of marketing messages accurately and efficiently—and they can adjust their messages accordingly.

The authors use a fictional company, Biz Ware, to describe how companies can map out an a grid a combination of the *attributes* (or variables) of a marketing message and the *levels* (or variations) of those attributes. Marketers can test a few combinations of those attributes and levels and can apply logistic regression analysis to extrapolate the probable customer responses to all the possible combinations. The company can then analyze the experiment's implications for its resources, revenues, and profitability. The authors also present the results of their work with Crayola, in which they used experimental design techniques to test that company's e-mail marketing campaign.

CONSUMERS ARE BOMBARDED daily with hundreds, perhaps thousands, of marketing messages. Delivered through all manner of media, from television commercials to telephone solicitations to supermarket circulars to Internet banner ads, these stimuli may elicit the desired response: The consumer clips a coupon, clicks on a link, or adds a product to a shopping cart. But the vast majority of marketing messages fail to hit their targets. Obviously, it would be valuable for companies to be able to anticipate which stimuli would prompt a response since even a small improvement in the browse-to-buy conversion rate can have a big impact on profitability. But it has been very difficult to isolate what drives consumer behavior, largely because there are so many possible combinations of stimuli.

Now, however, marketers have easier access, at relatively low cost, to experimental design techniques long applied in other fields such as pharmaceutical research. Experimental design, which quantifies the effects of independent stimuli on behavioral responses, can help marketing executives analyze how the various components of a marketing campaign influence consumer behavior. This approach is much more precise and cost effective than traditional market testing. And when you know how customers will respond to what you have to offer, you can target marketing programs directly to their needs—and boost the bottom line in the process.

Traditional Testing

The practice of testing various forms of a marketing or advertising stimulus isn't new. Direct marketers, in particular, have long used simple techniques such as split mailings to compare how customers react to different prices or promotional offers. But if they try to evaluate more than just a couple of campaign alternatives, traditional testing techniques quickly grow prohibitively expensive.

Consider the "test and control cell" method, which is the basis for almost all direct mail and e-commerce testing done today. It starts with a control cell for, say, a base price, then adds test cells for higher and lower prices. To test five price points, six promotions, four banner ad colors, and three ad placements, you'd need a control cell and 360 test cells ($5 \times 6 \times 4 \times 3 = 360$). And that's a relatively simple case. In credit card marketing, the possible combinations of brands, cobrands, annual percentage rates, teaser rates, marketing messages, and mail packaging can quickly add up to hundreds of thousands of possible bundles of attributes. Clearly, you cannot test them all.

There's another problem with this brute force approach: It typically does not reveal which individual variables are causing higher (or lower) responses from customers, since most control-cell tests reflect the combined effect of more than two simple variables. Is it the lower price that prompted the higher response? The promotional deal? The new advertising message? There's no way to know.

The problem has been magnified recently as companies have gained the ability to change their marketing stimuli much more quickly. Just a few years ago, changing prices and promotions on a few cans of food in the supermarket, for example, required the time-consuming application of sticky labels and the distribution of paper coupons. Today, a store can adjust prices and promotions electronically by simply reprogramming its checkout scanners. The Internet has further heightened marketing complexity by reducing the physical constraints on pricing, packaging, and communications. In the extreme, an on-line retailer could change the prices and promotion of every product it offers every minute of the day. It can also change the color of banner ads, the tone of promotional messages, and the content of outbound e-mails with relative ease.

The increasing complexity of the *stimulus-response network,* as we call it, means that marketers have more communication alternatives than ever before—and that the portion of alternatives they actually test is growing even smaller. But this greater complexity can also mean greater flexibility in your marketing programs—if you can uncover which changes in the stimulus-response network actually drive customer behavior. One way to do this is through scientific experimentation.

A New Marketing Science

The science of experimental design lets people project the impact of many stimuli by testing just a few of them. By using mathematical formulas to select and test a subset of combinations of variables that represent the complexity of all the original variables, marketers can model hundreds or even thousands of stimuli accurately and efficiently.

This is not the same thing as an after-the-fact analysis of consumer behavior, sometimes referred to as data mining. Experimental design is distinguished by the fact that you define and control the independent variables before putting them into the marketplace, trying out different kinds of stimuli on customers rather than observing them as they have naturally occurred. Because you control the introduction of stimuli, you can establish that differences in response can be attributed to the stimulus in question, such as packaging or color of a product, and not to other factors, such as limited availability of the product. In other words, experimental design reveals whether variables *caused* a certain behavior as opposed to simply being *correlated* with the behavior.

While experimental design itself isn't new, few marketing executives have used the technique—either because they haven't understood it or because day-to-day marketing operations have gotten in the way. But new technologies are making experimental design more accessible, more affordable, and easier to administer. (For more information on the genesis of this type of testing, see "The Origins of Experimental Design" at the end of this article) Companies today can collect detailed customer information much more easily than ever before and can use those data to build models that predict customer response with greater speed and accuracy.

Today's most popular experimental-design methods can be adapted and customized using guidelines from standard reference textbooks such as *Statistics for Experimenters* by George E. P. Box, J. Stuart Hunter, and William G. Hunter; and from off-the-shelf software packages such as the Statistical Analysis System, the primary product of SAS Institute. A handful of companies have already applied some form of experimental design to marketing. They include financial firms such as Chase, Household Finance, and Capital One, telecommunications provider Cable & Wireless, and Internet portal America Online.

Applying experimental-design methods requires business judgment and a degree of mathematical and statistical sophistication—both of which are well within the reach of most large corporations and many smaller organizations. The experimental design technique is particularly useful for companies that have large numbers of customers and that face rapid and constant change in their markets and product offers. Internet retailers, for instance, benefit greatly from experimentation because on-line customers tend to be fickle. Attracting browsers to a Web site and then converting them into buyers has proved very expensive and largely ineffective. Getting it right the first time is nearly impossible, so experimentation is critical. The rigorous and robust nature of experimental design, combined with the increasing challenges of marketing to oversaturated consumers, will make widespread adoption of this new marketing science only a matter of time in most industries.

The ABCs of Experimental Design

To illustrate how experimental design works, let's consider the following simple case. A company, which we'll call Biz Ware, is marketing a software product to other companies. Before launching a national campaign, Biz Ware wants to test three different variables, or *attributes*, of a sales message for the product: price, message, and promotion. Each of the three attributes can have a number of variations, or *levels*. Suppose the three attributes and their various levels are as shown in "Attributes and Levels of a Sales Message."

The total number of possible combinations can be determined by multiplying the number of levels of each attribute. The three attributes Biz Ware wants to test yield a total of 16 possible combinations since $4 \times 2 \times 2 = 16$. All 16 combinations can be mapped in the cells of a simple chart like "Biz Ware's Universe of Possible Combinations."

It's not necessary to test them all. Instead, using what's called a *fractional factorial design*, Biz Ware selects a subset of eight combinations to test.

"Factorial" means Biz Ware "crosses" each attribute (price, promotion, and message) with each of the others in gridlike fashion, as in the universe chart above. "Fractional" means Biz Ware then chooses a subset of those combinations in which the attributes are independent (either totally or partially) of each other. The following chart shows the resulting experimental design, with Xs marking the cells to be tested. Note that each level of each attribute is paired in at least one instance with each

level of the other attributes. So, for example, price at
$150 is matched at some point with each promotion and
each message. This makes it possible to unambiguously
separate the influence of each variable on customer
response. (See "Biz Ware's Experimental Design.")

The eight chosen combinations are now tested, using
one of several media: scripts at a call center, banner ads
on Biz Ware's Web site, e-mail messages to prospective
customers, and direct mail solicitations. (In general, you
should test using the medium you ultimately expect to
use for your marketing campaign, although you can also
choose multiple media and treat the choice of media as
an attribute in the experiment.)

Attributes and Levels of a Sales Message

	PRICE			
Level	(1)	(2)	(3)	(4)
	$150	$160	$170	$180

MESSAGE

(1) Speed

"Biz Ware lets you manage customer relationships in just minutes a day."

(2) Power

"Biz Ware can be expanded to handle a virtually infinite number of customer files."

PROMOTION

(1) 30-Day Trial

"You can try Biz Ware now for 30 days at no risk."

(2) Free Gift

"Buy Biz Ware now and receive our contact manager software absolutely free."

How big should the sample size be to make the experiment valid? The answer depends on several characteristics of the test and the target market. These may include the expected response rate, based on the results of past marketing efforts; the expected variation among subgroups of the market; and the complexity of the design, including the number of attributes and levels. In any event, the sample size should be large enough so that marketers can statistically detect the impact of the attributes on customer response. Since increasing the complexity and size of an experiment generally adds cost, marketers should determine the minimum sample size necessary to achieve a degree of precision that is

Biz Ware's Universe of Possible Combinations

Promotion	(1)	(1)	(2)	(2)
Message	(1)	(2)	(1)	(2)
Price (1)	X	X	X	X
Price (2)	X	X	X	X
Price (3)	X	X	X	X
Price (4)	X	X	X	X

Biz Ware's Experimental Design

Promotion	(1)	(1)	(2)	(2)
Message	(1)	(2)	(1)	(2)
Price (1)	X			X
Price (2)		X	X	
Price (3)		X	X	
Price (4)	X			X

useful for making business decisions. (There are standard guidelines in statistics that can help marketers answer the question of sample size.) We've conducted complex experiments by sending e-mail solicitations to lists of just 20,000 names, where 1,250 people each receive one of 16 stimuli.

Within a few days or weeks, the experiment's results come in. Biz Ware's marketers note the number and percentage of positive responses to each of the eight tested offers. (See "Biz Ware's Design Results.")

At a glance, you might intuitively understand that price has a significant impact on the response to the various offers, since the lower price offers (Price 1 and Price 2) generally drew much better response rates than the higher price offers (Price 3 and Price 4). But statistical modeling, using standard software, makes it possible to assess the impact of each variable with far greater precision. Indeed, by using a method known as *logistic regression analysis,* Biz Ware can extrapolate from the results of the experiment the probable response rates for all 16 cells. (See "Biz Ware's Modeled Responses.")

Note that the percentages shown below don't precisely match the original percentages from the test.

Biz Ware's Design Results

Promotion	(1)	(1)	(2)	(2)
Message	(1)	(2)	(1)	(2)
Price (1)	14%			40%
Price (2)		9%	13%	
Price (3)		6%	10%	
Price (4)	1%			7%

Biz Ware's Modeled Responses

Promotion	(1)	(1)	(2)	(2)
Message	(1)	(2)	(1)	(2)
Price (1)	14%	23%	28%	42%
Price (2)	7%	12%	15%	24%
Price (3)	3%	6%	7%	12%
Price (4)	1%	3%	3%	6%

That's because Biz Ware used the original percentages to create a general equation for estimating the results in all the cells. When the new equation is then applied to the cells already tested, the results usually vary somewhat from the original numbers. The important thing is that the tester ends up with a full set of consistent results for all possible permutations. (For more about how these calculations were made, see "Estimating a Response Model" at the end of this article.)

With this complete picture, it becomes clear that some combinations are far more likely to be effective than others. The combination of Price 1 ($150), Message 2 (Power), and Promotion 2 (Free Gift) is clearly the most attractive to consumers. But is it the right combination for Biz Ware? That's where business judgment comes in: The company's management will need to analyze the experiment's implications for its resources, revenue, and profitability.

Experimentation at Crayola

Let's look at an actual example of how experimental design can enhance a marketing campaign. Last year,

Crayola, a division of Binney & Smith and Hallmark, launched a creative arts and activities portal on the Internet called Crayola.com. The site's target customers include parents and educators, and it sells art supplies and offers arts-and-crafts project ideas and classroom lesson plans. We conducted an experimental design to help Crayola attract people to the site and convert browsers into buyers.

Based on Crayola's experience and market knowledge, we identified a set of stimuli that could be varied to drive traffic to Crayola.com and induce purchases. One of these stimuli was an e-mail to parents and teachers. To test various components of the e-mail content and format, we relied on the best judgment of Crayola's marketing staff about the messages that were most likely to appeal to the target markets. The e-mail included five key attributes that seemed likely to affect the customer response rate, which would be measured by click-throughs to the Crayola Web site. These attributes and their related levels were:

- **Two subject lines:** "Crayola.com Survey" and "Help Us Help You."

- **Three salutations:** "Hi [user name] :-)," "Greetings!" and "[user name]."

- **Two calls to action:** "As Crayola.com grows, we'd like to get your thoughts about the arts and how you use art materials" and "Because you as an educator have a special understanding of the arts and how art materials are used, we invite you to help build Crayola.com."

- **Three promotions:** "a chance to participate in a monthly drawing to win $100 worth of Crayola products; a monthly drawing for one of ten $25 Amazon.com gift certificates; and no promotion.

- **Two closings:** "Crayola.com" and "EducationEditor@Crayola.com."

Taking into account all the levels of each attribute, there were a total of 72 possible versions of the e-mail ($2 \times 3 \times 2 \times 3 \times 2 = 72$). While Crayola might have been able to test all 72 variations, the process would have been cumbersome and expensive. Instead, we created a subset of 16 e-mails to represent the 72 possible combinations. Over a two-week period, we sent the 16 types of e-mail to randomly selected samples of customers and tracked and analyzed their responses. The results were compelling. The "best" e-mail of the 72 possible scripts yielded a positive response rate of about 34% and was more than three times as effective at attracting parents as the "worst" e-mail, which yielded a positive response rate of only about 10%. (See "Crayola Draws Results" at the end of this article.) Among educators, the best e-mail script was nearly twice as effective as the worst script, with response rates of 35% for the best e-mail versus 20% for the worst.

We also conducted similar experiments with Crayola to test the effects of three different banner ads on the home page, as well as product, price, and promotions offered at the on-line store. The best combination was nearly four times as effective in converting shoppers into buyers as the worst combination and nearly doubled revenues per buyer.

Uncovering the Unexpected

In the Crayola experiments, as well as in other tests, our results have yielded surprising insights. When we ask experienced marketers to predict which stimuli are likely to elicit the best responses, few get it right. Crayola, for example, was surprised to find that a price reduction on a product or line of products generated sufficient volume to create higher revenues while also maintaining the site's profitability. Conventional wisdom would have suggested that raising prices would be a more effective way to increase revenue.

Of course, the findings from tests like these can't be generalized. For instance, compare the e-mail tests we conducted at Crayola with similar tests we performed for Cable & Wireless. At Crayola, e-mails containing no promotional offer drew poorly compared with e-mails containing either of the two promotional offers tested (a $100 product drawing and a $25 Amazon.com gift certificate). At Cable & Wireless, though, e-mails with no promotional offer drew the *best* click-through rate. But that's part of the value of experimental design: It allows marketers to move beyond rules of thumb or experience to pinpoint the marketing approaches that work best with a particular audience in a particular marketplace at a particular moment in time.

The Expanding Marketing Universe

In the world of marketing experimentation, the Crayola tests are relatively simple. We tested only a handful of marketing attributes, with a relatively small number of levels for each. Even so, the customer impact was impressive, with the best combinations of stimuli drawing double, triple, or quadruple response rates compared with the worst combinations.

The approach we took with Crayola can be extended and applied to more attributes and more levels. It's not unusual for a company to test ten or more attributes, including some with as many as eight levels. A credit card company, for example, might be interested in testing six teaser rates, six cobrands, four different annual percentage rates, six promotions, four insurance packages, four modes of communication, eight direct mail packages, and four mailing schedules. This represents a possible set of 442,368 distinct marketing stimuli, obviously too large a universe for a test-and-control-cell approach. But by using experimental design to select and test a manageable number—say 128 combinations of these variables—the credit card company could estimate with great accuracy the customer reaction to all 442,368 combinations.

And this is by no means the upper limit of the usefulness of experimental design. The responses being sought from customers can be more complex as well. Customers may have multiple options to choose from rather than a simple "yes" or "no" response—for example, a choice between one-year, two-year, and three-year subscriptions or no purchase.

Different types of experimental designs can be used when the experimental objectives vary. For example, so-called *screening designs* can efficiently test very large numbers of attributes to select a smaller number to investigate in more detail. Subsequent testing can employ more levels for each of a smaller collection of attributes. *Response surface designs* are used in food testing in which multiple dimensions such as sweet, salty, crunchy, and sour have an ideal level somewhere between "too much" and "not enough." The design lets testers estimate the ideal combination of tastes and textures.

Getting Results

Naturally, there are limits to the power of experimental design. This approach requires thoughtful planning to hypothesize what you are looking for and to rule out other possibilities before the experiment can begin.

One caution is that many experimental designs rely on "main effects" models. That is, they assume that interaction effects—the impact that one variable can have on another variable—are negligible. This is usually a reasonable assumption when you're dealing with complex combinations of three, four, and five variables at a time. However, interactions between two variables can be important and can be tested. For example, suppose you find that free samples have a more positive impact on a product's sales than do coupons. You may also learn that free samples provide an even greater lift when they are handed out in the stores as opposed to being sent through the mail. One variable, the chosen distribution channel, interacts meaningfully with another variable, the promotion itself.

Experimental design also calls for substantive knowledge to frame the problem, careful application of theoretically sound methods, and skillful interpretation of the results in the appropriate context. Some knowledge of basic statistical methods is necessary, of course. But even more important is a nuanced understanding of customers and the ability to form reasonable assumptions concerning which attributes and levels should be tested and which shouldn't. Experimental design should be one part of a continuous test-and-learn cycle.

Marketing is, and always will be, a creative endeavor. But it doesn't have to be so mysterious. As marketing noise and advertising clutter continue to increase, marketers will find that scientific experimentation will allow them to better communicate with their customers—and substantially raise the odds that their marketing efforts will pay off.

The Origins of Experimental Design

EXPERIMENTAL DESIGN METHODOLOGIES—some dating as far back as the nineteenth century—have been used for years across many fields, including process manufacturing, psychology, and pharmaceutical clinical trials, and they are well known to most statisticians. Sir Ronald A. Fisher was among the first statisticians to introduce the concepts of randomization and analysis of variance. In the early 1900s, he worked at the Rothamsted Agricultural Experimental Station outside London. His focus was on increasing agricultural yields.

Another major breakthrough in the field came with the work of U.S. economist and Nobel laureate Daniel L. McFadden in the 1970s, who drew on psychological theories to explain that consumer choices are a function of the available alternatives and other consumer characteristics. In helping to design San Francisco's BART commuter rail system, McFadden analyzed the way people evaluate trade-offs in travel time and cost and how those trade-offs affect their decisions about means of transportation. He was able to help forecast demand for BART and determine where best to locate stations. The model was quite accurate, predicting a 6.4% share of commuter travel for BART, which was close to the actual 6.2% share the system achieved.

Estimating a Response Model

LOGISTIC REGRESSION ANALYSIS is a statistical technique that allows an experimenter to analyze the impact of each stimulus in an experiment. The formula assumes that the outcome—in Biz Ware's case, the customer response rate—is a function of the attributes—in Biz Ware's case, price, message, and promotion. Here's what Biz Ware's generic equation looks like:

$$\text{Log}\left(\frac{\text{response rate}}{1-\text{response rate}}\right) = a + b_1 \text{ (price)} + b_2 \text{ (message)} + b_3 \text{ (promotion)}$$

We plug Biz Ware's customer response data into this equation, using SAS software to estimate the coefficients (a, b_1, b_2, and b_3). For price we can drop a number into the formula. For message and promotion, which are qualitative attributes, we assign a dummy code—zero or one, since there are only two levels for each attribute. It does not matter which attribute is assigned which number. For Biz Ware, the equation looks like this:

$$\text{Log}\left(\frac{\text{response rate}}{1-\text{response rate}}\right) = 10.3 - 8.1 \text{ (price)} + 0.6 \text{ (message)} + 0.9 \text{ (promotion)}$$

The coefficients tell us a few things: Higher price has a negative impact on demand (hence, the coefficient b_1 is –8.1) and the effect of promotion is greater than the effect of message (because 0.9 is greater than 0.6). But more important, these coefficients allow us to apply the equation to extrapolate from the data collected and predict responses for all 16 cells.

Crayola Draws Results

Sample E-mail

Crayola.com marketers wanted to measure how customer response would be affected by different variations (or levels) of five main e-mail attributes: two subjects, three salutations, two calls to action, three promotions, and two closings. "Sample E-mail" shows one of the 72 possible combinations. An experimental design was developed so that only 16 combinations had to be tested.

Parents' Response Rates

The company measured the responses it received and through statistical modeling could quickly pinpoint which stimuli appealed most to its target customers—in this case, parents.

Sample E-mail

Subject	Help Us Help You
Salutation	Greetings!
Call to Action	Because you as an educator have a special understanding of the arts and how art materials are used, we invite you to help build Crayola.com. By answering ten quick questions, you'll be helping to make sure improvements we make to Crayola.com meet your needs. Simply follow this link: http://_____. (If this does not work, please cut and paste the link into your browser's address bar.)
Promotion	As a thank you, you will be entered into our monthly drawing to win one of ten $25 Amazon.com gift certificates. By completing our survey, you'll be automatically entered. Thanks for your assistance. Be sure to check back often for new fun, creative, and colorful ideas and solutions.
Closing	Yours, Crayola.com

The subject line "Crayola.com Survey," for example, was more effective at creating positive responses than "Help Us Help You." The response rate of the former was 7.5% higher than that of the latter, all else being equal. (See "Parents' Response Rates.")

Parents' Response Rates

	Levels	Change in Response Rate
Subject	Crayola.com Survey	7.5%
	Help Us Help You	0.0%
Salutation	Hi [user name]:-)	2.7%
	Greetings!	0.0%
	[user name]	3.4%
Call to Action	As Crayola.com grows. . .	0.0%
	Because you are. . .	3.5%
Promotion	$100 product drawing	8.4%
	$25 Amazon.com gift certificate drawing	5.2%
	No offer	0.0%
Closing	Crayola.com	0.0%
	EducationEditor@Crayola.com	1.2%

Script Attributes

The combination of attributes that got the best response from parents was more than three times as effective as the combination of attributes that got the worst response. "Script Attributes" shows the best and worst script attributes of the 72 possible combinations.

Script Attributes

	Best Response	Worst Response
Subject	Crayola.com Survey	Help Us Help You
Salutation	User name	Greetings!
Call to Action	Because you are. . .	As Crayola.com grows. . .
Promotion	$100 product drawing	No offer
Closing	EducationEditor@Crayola.com	Crayola.com
Response Rate	33.7%	9.7%

The best script is 3.5 times more effective than the worst.

Originally published in October 2001
Reprint R0109K

About the Contributors

DAVID A. AAKER is the vice-chairman of Prophet, a brand strategy consultancy, and Professor Emeritus of Marketing Strategy at the Haas School of Business, University of California, Berkeley. The winner of the Paul D. Converse Award for Outstanding Contributions to the Development of the Science of Marketing and the Vijay Mahajan Award for Career Contributions to Marketing Strategy, Professor Aaker has published over eighty articles and eleven books including "Strategic Market Management," "Managing Brand Equity," *Building Strong Brands,* and *Brand Leadership*, coauthored with Erich Joachimsthaler. His books have been translated into twelve languages. Cited as one of the most quoted authors in marketing, Professor Aaker has won awards for the best article in the *California Management Review* and *The Journal of Marketing.*

ERIC ALMQUIST is a vice president and member of the Board of Directors of Mercer Management Consulting. He specializes in customer-focused business strategies. His work has focused on corporate brand strategy development, development of branded value propositions, marketing experimentation, and customer relationship management. Dr. Almquist has contributed to such publications as the *Harvard Business Review, Journal of Brand Management, Marketing Research, Journal of Economic History*, and *Economic History Review*. He speaks regularly on the topics of customer-driven strategies and corporate brand strategies and is a trustee of the Marketing Science Institute.

At the time this article was originally published, MARK E. BERGEN was an associate professor of marketing at the University of Minnesota's Carlson School of Management in Minneapolis.

STEPHEN BROWN is professor of marketing research at the University of Ulster, Northern Ireland. The author or coeditor of twelve books, including *Postmodern Marketing, Romancing the Market,* and *Marketing: The Retro Revolution,* Professor Brown has been a visiting professor at Northwestern University, the University of Utah, and the University of California, Irvine, among others.

SCOTT DAVIS is the principal and founder of Strategic Marketing Decisions and consults on pricing and marketing issues to a variety of international industries, including medical equipment, telecommunications, and packaged goods. His clients range in size from new business start-ups to *Fortune* 500 companies. The author of several articles, his research has appeared in the *Journal of Marketing Research, Journal of Retailing,* and other well-known publications. He has received awards for his teaching and research, and has served as a reviewer for a number of scholarly journals. He currently teaches pricing for the Haas School of Business at the University of California, Berkeley and internet marketing for Graduate School of Management at the University of California, Davis.

MARY JO HATCH is a professor of commerce at the McIntire School of Commerce, University of Virginia. Prior to this appointment she held positions at Cranfield School of Management, the Copenhagen Business School, UCLA, and San Diego State University. Her main area of research is corporate branding, and she has published related articles on organizational culture, organizational symbolism, and organizational identity and image. She is the author of *Organization Theory* and the coeditor of *The Expressive Organization*, with Majken Schultz and Mogens Holten Larsen. She can be contacted at mjhatch@virginia.edu.

At the time this article was originally published, MANNIE JACKSON was the owner and chairman of the Harlem Globetrotters.

ERICH JOACHIMSTHALER, a published thought leader on global brand strategy, is founder and CEO of The Brand Leadership Company, and consults to executives at many of the world's leading companies. He is the author of more than forty articles and case studies in leading academic and business journals, including *Harvard Business Review*, *Sloan Management Review*, *Business Week*, and *MIS Quarterly*, and his book *Brand Leadership*, coauthored with David A. Aaker, is considered a groundbreaking discussion on the current revolution in brand strategy. A sought-after speaker, he conducts executive-level conferences and workshops around the world in English, German, and Spanish. In addition to his consulting work, Mr. Joachimsthaler conducts extensive research on global brands. He is a visiting professor of business administration at the Darden Graduate School of Business Administration, University of Virginia and has held academic positions at the University of Southern California and at I.E.S.E. in Barcelona.

KEVIN LANE KELLER is the E. B. Osborn Professor of Marketing at the Amos Tuck School of Business at Dartmouth College. An academic pioneer in the study of integrated marketing communications and brand equity, Professor Keller has served as brand confidant to marketers for some of the world's most successful brands, including Disney, Ford, Intel, Levi Strauss, Nike, Procter & Gamble, and Starbucks. He is also the author of *Strategic Brand Management*. Professor Keller's academic résumé includes degrees from Cornell, Duke, and Carnegie Mellon universities, award-winning research, and an eight-year stint on the faculty at the Stanford Business School, where he served as the head of the marketing group.

DAVID KENNY, chairman and Chief Executive Officer of Digitas, is one of the chief architects of global eBusiness transformation in the Internet age. With perspective and insight, he has earned a coveted role as strategic partner to some of the world's most respected corporations, including American Express, AT&T, General Motors, Charles Schwab, Delta Air Lines, FedEx, L.L. Bean, Morgan Stanley Dean Witter, and the National Basketball Association. A former senior partner at Bain & Company, the global strategic consulting firm, Mr. Kenny holds a BS from the General Motors Institute and an MBA from the Harvard Business School. He is chairman of the board of Teach for America, and a director of Harvard Business School Publishing and The Corporate Executive Board. He is also an active member of the BOLD Diversity Initiative.

JOHN F. MARSHALL is senior vice president and Global Head of the Digital Strategy group at Digitas, where his responsibilities include partnering with clients to determine how to use the Internet and emerging technologies to create new business models geared toward gaining competitive advantage. Mr. Marshall also leads the Digitas Wireless Practice, and is responsible for the strategy and implementation of customer solutions for the "ubiquitous Internet" for the firm's clients. Prior to joining Digitas in 1999, Mr. Marshall had twelve years of experience in strategic consulting and technology investment banking. He was most recently a partner at MercerDelta Management Consulting. His current focus has been on corporate strategy development for *Fortune* 100 companies, with particular emphasis on designing new business models in response to major changes in technology. Mr. Marshall has worked extensively with companies such as AT&T, Sears, and Dow Chemical to define new customer-driven business models. A former venture capitalist and technology analyst, he has significant experience in capital markets, new technology venture development, and value-based management.

AKSHAY R. RAO is the Carlson Term Professor of Marketing at the University of Minnesota's Carlson School of Management. A winner of the Ferber award for Interdisciplinary Research from the *Journal of Consumer Research*, and the Maynard award for Marketing Theory from the *Journal of Marketing*, Professor Rao has published several highly influential articles on pricing, marketing strategy, and consumer behavior in the premier marketing journals. He has held visiting positions at the Sloan School at MIT and at the Hong Kong University of Science & Technology. Professor Rao's teaching, research, and consulting emphasize consumer behavior, pricing strategy, product/brand management, and sales force management. His views are regularly solicited by local and national media in print, radio, and television, including the *Wall Street Journal*, the MacNeil/Lehrer News Hour on PBS, and CNN.

MAJKEN SCHULTZ is a professor at Copenhagen Business School. Her research interests cross the disciplines of organizational behavior, marketing, and strategy and include both theoretical and managerial issues relevant to identity, corporate branding, and reputation management. She has published numerous articles in leading international journals focusing on organizational studies, management, and marketing. She is the author or editor of several books, including *The Expressive Organization*. Professor Schultz works as a part-time consultant for LEGO Company and serves as a board member of Danske Bank, Foreningen, RealDanmark, and the Carl Bro Group. She is also director of the Reputation Institute, Denmark (www.reputationinstitute.com).

DR. GORDON WYNER, a vice president of Mercer Management Consulting, focuses his work on understanding customer priorities, preferences, and economic value as a basis for successful business design. He assists clients in developing and executing strategies for selecting customers and creating value propositions that are optimally configured to customer requirements and realize value from customer relationships through acquisition, management, and retention programs. Dr. Wyner has consulted with clients in a broad range of industries, including communications, information, entertainment, financial services, transportation, and consumer products. He has also developed new methods and capabilities for segmentation, value proposition design, and targeting using customer databases, surveys, and market experiments. A regular columnist for *Marketing Management* and *Marketing Research* magazines, Dr. Wyner is a frequent contributor to various industry publications and speaks at numerous conferences. He is on the Board of Trustees and is chairman of the executive committee of the Marketing Science Institute.

Index